The Laments of Jeremiah and Their Contexts

THE SOCIETY OF BIBLICAL LITERATURE
MONOGRAPH SERIES

Adela Yarbro Collins, Editor
E.F. Campbell, Associate Editor

Number 42
THE LAMENTS OF JEREMIAH AND THEIR CONTEXTS
A Literary and Redactional Study of Jeremiah 11-20

by
Mark S. Smith

Mark S. Smith

THE LAMENTS OF JEREMIAH
AND THEIR CONTEXTS
A Literary and Redactional Study
of Jeremiah 11-20

Scholars Press
Atlanta, Georgia

THE LAMENTS OF JEREMIAH AND THEIR CONTEXTS

by
Mark S. Smith

©1990
The Society of Biblical Literature

Library of Congress Cataloging in Publication Data

Smith, Mark S., 1955-
    The laments of Jeremiah and their contexts : A Literary and
    Redactional Study of Jeremiah 11-20 / Mark
    S. Smith.
    p. cm. -- (Monograph series / the Society of Biblical
    Literature ; no. 42)
    Includes bibliographical references and indexes.
    ISBN 1-55540-460-X. -- ISBN 1-5540-461-8 (pbk.)
    1. Bible. O.T. Lamentations XI-XX--Criticism, interpretation,
etc. I. Title. II. Series: Monograph series (Society of Biblical
Literature) ; no. 42.
BS1535.2.S55 1990
224'.2066-dc20   90-39340
                                             CIP

Printed in the United States of America
on acid-free paper

For Benjamin Bloch Smith and Rachel Elizabeth Smith

I led them with cords of compassion,
with bands of love...
and I bent down to them and fed them.

—Hosea 11:4

Today is gone. Today was fun.
Tomorrow is another one.
Every day,
from here to there,
funny things are everywhere.

—Dr. Seuss, *One fish two fish red fish blue fish*

Table of Contents

—❧❧—

Acknowledgements

This short work initially took form as two public presentations. Chapter One was the result of a generous invitation to deliver lectures on the major prophets at the Saint Paul Seminary/School of Divinity of the College of Saint Thomas. The occasion of the lectures provided me with an opportunity to rekindle friendships with my former colleagues at Saint Paul Seminary. I taught at the Seminary from 1984 to 1986, and the warmth and kindness of its staff and students frequently grace my memory. I thank Charles Froehle, Rector/Vice-President of the Seminary/School of Divinity, and Deans Vic Klimoski and Art Zannoni for making possible my return. These friends and others, too numerous to list, made our family visit memorable.

Much of the material in Chapters Two and Three was presented at the Prophetic Literature section of the national meeting of the Society of Biblical Literature in 1988. Following the meeting, I had the pleasure of communicating with both Pete Diamond and Kathleen O'Connor about this short study. Since their works treating Jeremiah's laments in context (Diamond 1987; O'Connor 1988) provided the point of departure for Chapters Two and Three, their reactions to this study were most welcome, and I wish to thank both scholars for their comments and encouragement. I am also grateful to Edward F. Campbell, Jr. and the two scholars for the SBLMS series who served as readers for this work. They offered numerous suggestions which improved the quality of this study. I thank Stephen Cook for his help in proofreading.

I also wish to thank the Whitney Humanities Center of Yale University for providing a good second home that helped me bring this study to completion. Thanks to the Whitney Humanities Center, I was granted a leave from one part of the university to savor many varieties of exotic growth in other parts of the university.

Finally, this exposition is dedicated with great affection and love to my children, Benjamin and Rachel. This work belonged to their early years. Daily they tell me secrets.

Abbreviations

The abbreviations standard to the SBL monograph series are used, with the following additions:

Joüon   P. Joüon, *Grammaire de l'hébreu biblique.* Édition photomécanique corrigée. Rome: Institut Biblique Pontifical, 1965. cited by paragraph.

KTU   M. Dietrich, O. Loretz and J. Sanmartín, *Die keilalphabetischen Texte aus Ugarit.* Alter Orient und Altes Testament 24/1. Kevelaer: Verlag Butzon & Bercker; Neukirchen-Vluyn: Neukirchener Verlag, 1976. cited by text number.

NJB   *The New Jerusalem Bible.* London: Darton, Longman & Todd, 1985.

NJPS   *Tanakh - The Holy Scriptures; The New JPS According to the Traditional Hebrew Text.* Philadelphia/New York/Jerusalem: The Jewish Publication Society, 1988.

//   Poetic parallel terms.

*   Theoretical form.

Introduction

Following Duhm's commentary on Jeremiah in 1901, numerous scholars have isolated the "laments of Jeremiah" from their immediate contexts (see Diamond 1987:11-18). This interpretive move, inspired by the form-critical features of the laments, has rarely inspired a comparable effort to reintegrate them into their settings. Stated differently, assuming the originally independent character of the laments, how and why did the laments come to assume their positions within Jeremiah 11-20? Some scholars have tried to relate the laments to their immediate contexts. Two in particular have recently examined the relationship between the laments of Jeremiah and their contexts within Jeremiah 11-20. Following the lead of scholars such as Rudolph (1968) and Thiel (1973), Diamond (1987:149-88) and O'Connor (1988:97-113) noted detailed links between the laments and their immediate contexts on the level of word-links (*Stichworte*), images and themes.[1] Diamond (1987) and O'Connor (1988) also studied the laments in terms of their differing perceptions of the literary arrangements contained in chapters 11-20.

These studies address what may be the fundamental conundrum of Jeremiah 11-20, namely the nature of the redacted context of the laments. In general, there are two basic views on this issue which apply to the book of Jeremiah as a whole (for surveys of literature, see Hyatt 1951:71-95; Thiel 1973:3-31; Childs 1979:339-54; Carroll 1986:33-86; Brueggemann 1987; Seitz 1989a). Enjoying a long venerable tradition, one approach attributes to the historical Jeremiah or his disciple, Baruch, primary authorship of at least most of the material (Skinner 1922; Leclerq 1954; Blank 1961; Bright 1965:lxxxvi-cxviii; Lundbom 1975; Holladay 1986;

---

[1] See chapter three for further details.

Unterman 1987; cf. Ittman 1981; for further examples, see Vermeylen 1981:271 n. 1). Therefore, the picture of Jeremiah and the events in his life can be reasonably drawn on the basis of the book (cf. Wilson 1980:233-51). The laments then are taken as personal expressions of Jeremiah in the face of great opposition to his prophetic ministry.

A second scholarly approach attributes the organization and shape of the book less to either the man, Jeremiah, or his scribal disciple, Baruch. Largely following the lead of Duhm (1901), Mowinckel (1914) identified much of the material surrounding the laments in chapters 11-20 as Deuteronomistic; he grouped the Deuteronomistic material as part of what he called the "C" source. Many modern commentators have built on Mowinckel's observations by arguing that the book involved a major Deuteronomistic redaction (Bright 1951:30-55; Hyatt 1951; Rudolph 1968; Thiel 1973, 1981; Tov 1972:196-99, 1981, 1985; Wilson 1980:231-33; Ahuis 1982; Carroll 1986; 1989:21-30; McKane 1986; Seitz 1989a; 1989b:1-6, 223-35; cf. Duhm 1901, esp. xvi-xx; Cornhill 1905; Volz 1928). This line of interpretation operates on the premise that the book constitutes a highly complicated and multi-leveled body of material, which was given its present form and internal sets of referentiality largely by Deuteronomistic editors (cf. Weippert 1973) who viewed Jeremiah as standing in the line of prophets like Moses (Deut 18:15-22; see Holladay 1964; 1966; Wilson 1980:237-40; Ahuis 1982:76-77; Levenson 1984; Seitz 1989a).

Text-critical considerations bear directly on theories about the book's redactional history. As Seitz (1989b:214 n. 16) comments, "especially in the case of Jeremiah, where a decidedly shorter and differently arranged text exists in the LXX, text analysis begins to merge with redactional analysis." The work of Tov (1972:189-99; 1981; 1985) proceeds in exactly this fashion. Tov posits two Deuteronomistic redactions on the basis of the shorter text of LXX and 4QJer[b] (subtracting its own further additions) and the longer text of the MT. In other words, LXX and 4QJer[b] (not counting their own internal additions unattested in the MT) reflect one edition of the book, and MT represents a second edition. Furthermore, Tov (1985:230) and Stulman (1986:146) highlight the heavily Deuteronomistic character of the first edition. They also note that the second edition is less heavily Deuteronomistic. In Tov's words,

> The larger part of the Deuteronomistic stratum is found in edition I, but editor II added many Deuteronomistic phrases and also complete sections such as 11:7-8. Editor II may have been one of the last members of that ill-defined "Deuteronomistic school," or else he simply imitated its style.

The second edition involves a number of additions which provide some insight into its character. Varughese (1984:127, 135, 177, 181-186, 188) notes that (besides 16:1) expansions in MT 11:7-8, 16:4, 17:1-4 and 20:5 are not found in LXX. These prosaic additions exhibit a Deuteronomistic perspective and language of judgement against Israel (Diamond 1987:188). Similarly, comparisons between MT and LXX in Jer 15:1 and 16:13 reflect the same stress on irrevocable judgement in MT in a way conspicuously different from LXX 15:1 and 16:13. LXX to 15:1 presupposes *ʾlyhm* instead of MT *ʾl-hᶜm hzh*. According to Varughese (1984:200; cf. Janzen 1973:74), the MT phrase in this verse

> suggests that even if Moses and Samuel interceded, Yahweh will not turn to the people in mercy or compassion. The OG [Old Greek] *Vorlage* could be understood in a different sense. Even if these ancient figures interceded on behalf of the people, Yahweh will not turn *to them* (i.e. Moses and Samuel) to recognize their appeal. His decision is final.

The MT and LXX variants to 16:13 reflect a similar pronounced judgement against Israel. Varughese (1984:203) suggests that LXX *lᵖ ytnw (dosousin) lkm hnynh* reflects the notion that foreign deities cannot respond to the exilees, while MT *lᵖ ʾtn lkm hnynh* presents Yahweh denying any favor to the exilees. Hence the MT renderings of these passages as well as the standardization of superscriptions represented by 16:1 reflect an attempt to orient further the Jeremianic material in chapters 11-20 toward the basic theme of judgement. Indeed, the prophetic laments in these chapters are ultimately subordinate to this purpose (Diamond 1987:183). This is not to imply that judgement reflects a slant added only late to the Jeremianic corpus. On the contrary, judgement appears at a variety of stages in the corpus, and the material added later in MT accents this traditional theme. For example, the Deuteronomistic prose sections in 11:1f., 13:1f., 16:1f., and 18:1f. (Stulman 1986:63-70, 73-76) focusing on judgement are largely preserved in LXX. Hence the shorter version of Jeremiah, which many scholars regard as largely an older edition of the book (Tov 1981; Stulman 1986), bore a heavily Deuteronomistic redaction. The later redaction of Jeremiah, represented by the MT, was also largely Deuteronomistic in a number of its additions.

Carroll (1989:23, 77) would attribute a further feature to the second edition of the book. There are a number of instances where the second edition adds the phrase "Jeremiah the prophet," which makes the figure the referent of the material. This feature belongs, according to Carroll, to the tendency in the second edition to place the material in the life of the prophet, to historicize it. Carroll (1989:77) claims, in part on the basis of this feature, that "perhaps the figure of Jeremiah is more the creation of tradition than the creator of it." This claim is perhaps overstated. Moreover, Carroll's view has little bearing on the questions of chapters 11-20 since the second edition adds this phrase in chapters 11-20 only in 20:2. In sum, the text-critical evidence points to two Deuteronomistic editions of the book (Janzen 1973; Soderlund 1985: esp. 246-48; cf. Tov 1972, 1981, 1985; Varughese 1984). The great variety of form-critical material in Jeremiah 11-20 and the complex text-critical evidence for the MT and LXX forms of the book suggest that Jeremiah was a heavily redacted work.

The redacted character of Jeremiah suggests examining the laments not only in isolation, but also within their larger context in chapters 11-20. While the approach of Carroll (1986) has the effect of unnecessarily severing the tradition of Jeremianic material from the figure of the prophet, it has the merit of taking seriously the later redaction. Indeed, the variations attested between MT and LXX versions point to the heavily redacted character of the book, although it needs to be noted that the date of the "first edition" of the book, to use Tov's expression (1981, 1985), reflected in the shorter text of LXX and 4QJer[b], could be quite early. How early is unknown. Childs (1979:344) ventures a date from the seventh century to the exile for the so-called "C source" passages isolated by Mowinckel (1914). This view would imply that the exile represents the *terminus a quo* for the formation of the "first edition." Childs' dating of "C" seems to be based on the similarities of its language with other Deuteronomistic works. However, this criterion could support either an exilic or post-exilic date for the formation of the "first edition." The heavily Deuteronomistic character of some post-exilic compositions such as Nehemiah 9 and parts of the Temple Scroll (11QT) (see Levine 1978; Yadin 1983; Stegemann 1983a:156-57; 1983b:507 n. 37, 515-16; 1985:409; Callaway 1986) would militate against using Deuteronomistic language to support an exilic dating for the "first edition." In view of the internal redaction of the laments with the Deuteronomistic material, a post-exilic dating appears plausible.

Internal evidence may be marshalled to support an exilic or post-exilic "first edition." Noting Neh 13:15-18 as the closest parallel in content and diction to Jer 17:19-27, numerous commentators (Carroll 1986:368; Holladay 1986:509; McKane 1986:417-18) interpret it as post-exilic. For example, Overholt (1986:623) comments that the passage appears to be a rather late priestly attempt to defend current religious and political practice by linking failure to observe the Sabbath to the national catastrophe of 585 B.C. and by justifying the absence of a king in post-exilic Israel.

Weinfeld (1976:55) offers two reasons for dating this piece to the post-exilic period. First, this section is addressed to kings rather than to one monarch and is therefore a post-exilic indictment of Judean kings in general (cf. Jer 19:3). This evidence is not in itself persuasive, as the mention of kings could conceivably apply to the end of the Judean monarchy, a period involving several contemporary royal figures (see Seitz 1989b:80-100, 117, 136). Second, the positive ideas expressed about the Sabbath in this section seem to run counter to the cultic criticisms expressed in Jer 7:21-23. Since this passage appears in both MT and LXX, it would appear to belong to the "first edition," which if the dating of the passage is correct, would point to an exilic or post-exilic setting. Other evidence for post-exilic redaction have been offered (e.g., Vermeylen 1981; Carroll 1986), though without precise evidence for dating.

The complicated form-critical and text-critical character of chapters 11-20 has directly affected the debate over Jeremiah's authorship of the material in these chapters, including the laments. According to Carroll, the laments are so formulaic that a disciple of Jeremiah or a later editor of this material could have formulated these words in the knowledge that the prophet's ministry caused him to lament. Pohlmann (1989) interprets the laments as post-exilic compositions expressing an eschatological hope in divine intervention.

There appears to be some basis for arguing for a pre-exilic date for the laments, nonetheless. Thiel (1973:162-63) and Seitz (1989b:89) cite Jer 12:7-13, 13:15-27, 14:2-9, 17-22 and 15:5-9 as examples of authentic material dating to the end of the Judean monarchy. Seitz (1989b:98, 100, 101, 103, 294; cf. 160-61) would place the non-Deuteronomistic oracles of chapters 9-15 in the context of the events leading to the initial deportation in 597. Some material within chapters 11-20 alludes to historical events of Jeremiah's day or addresses historical personages known from the life of the prophet. Although this fact does not demonstrate that every non-Deuteronomistic passage in chapters 11-20 is Jeremianic, historical references in non-Deuteronomistic passages in these chapters give weight to their authenticity. Following O'Connor and other scholars who venture remarks bearing on the prophet's life, the laments may be imputed to the prophet despite some scholarly caution to the contrary. Jeremiah's authorship of the laments (discounting discernible additions) cannot be established beyond doubt, but the placement of the laments within chapters 11-20 and their largely non-Deuteronomistic character support the dating of these compositions to the life of Jeremiah. Besides the problem that no proof can be adduced, there is no compelling reason not to place them within the prophet's ministry. Given the difficulty inherent in proving Jeremiah's authorship of the laments, they should not be used, however, to create overarching reconstructions of the prophet's life. Whether the prophet or a disciple authored the laments, they indicate that the prophet's mission met with resistance. The complex variety of material and divergencies in the textual traditions urge caution against proceeding to substantial and extensive historical reconstructions of the prophet's life. At the same time, there is a significant reason for recognizing at least in a minimal way the original function of the laments. The laments' original purpose conspicuously contrasts with, and therefore highlights, their additional functions in their redactional context.

This essay examines the laments and their contexts with the purpose of offering preliminary observations about their literary relations. There are two main reasons for this study. The first is to re-orient the discussion of the laments. Rather than treat chapters 11-20 primarily from the perspective of the laments, this study treats separately the laments in isolation and chapters 11-20 as a whole. More specifically, in order to appreciate fully the laments and their larger contexts, the study of verbal and thematic links which Diamond and O'Connor draw between the laments and their immediate contexts is extended more fully to various units in chapters 11-20. Indeed, there is a particular need to examine more precisely the literary and redactional relations between the laments and their contexts. The linguistic and literary interplay within the laments and their contexts creates additional meaning and purpose for the laments. The works of McKane (1986:1-lxxxiii) and other scholars are helpful for attempting to indicate the relations between various parts despite their disparate origins. McKane (1986:xcii) perhaps wisely demurs from an attempt to generalize about the theology of the book, but his concept of a "rolling corpus" provides some guidelines for venturing a synthetic view of the laments in context. The second reason for this study revolves around delineating the larger units within chapters 11-20 and the nature of the arrangement of the material. The demarcation of the larger units plays a significant role in the interpretation of the laments by Diamond and O'Connor, but their definitions of the major units do not coincide. Addressing these two issues requires a substantial presentation of both the laments and their contexts. Accordingly, the emphasis in this study falls on describing the literary relations between the laments and their contexts with the purpose of rendering some order from, in McKane's words (1986:xlix), "the untidy and desultory nature of the aggregation of material which comprises the book of Jeremiah." With respect to chapters 11-20, it may be possible to strike some middle point between Thiel's comprehensive approach (1973; see Chapter Two below) and McKane's "rolling corpus" (1986:l-lxxxiii). Stated differently, it is necessary to ask how the relationship among the whole and its parts was perceived at various stages. Indeed, the parts derived from different levels of the tradition extending from the prophet himself through the second Deuteronomistic edition of the book.

Chapter One treats the laments individually, with reference to some of their features. The works by Diamond (1987:21-125) and O'Connor (1988:7-96) provide detailed analysis of the laments. Rather than duplicate either their efforts or the labors of three recent commentaries on Jeremiah (Carroll 1986; Holladay 1986; McKane 1986), only some basic remarks on the laments are offered in Chapter One. Diamond and O'Connor overlap in their reconstructions for the original function of the laments. While noting the difficulties in reconstructing the original function of the laments based on their content, Diamond (1987:33-35, 50-51, 77-78, 81, 100, 113-14, 122-25, 127-91, 212 n. 46; 1989:696) and O'Connor (1988:26, 42, 50, 58, 71-72, 85-96, 97, 103) conclude that one function original to the laments was to justify Jeremiah's prophetic mission in the face of opposition. A basic presentation of the laments is necessary for this study, since many thematic and verbal connections between the laments and their contexts provide the key to understanding the relations among the two sets of material.

Chapter Two deals with two issues: first, the larger units within Jeremiah 11-20, one of the most difficult issues in the interpretation of this section of the book; and second, the arrangement of material within these larger units. The interpretation of the laments ultimately depends on describing their larger setting, and determination of this setting depends partially on delineating the units to which they belong. After some consideration of the historical and literary difficulties, the delineation of units by both Diamond and O'Connor is rejected. Neither author devotes attention to the variety and functions of the superscriptions. Mostly based on the superscriptions, it would appear that the units within chapters 11-20 are neither 11-13, 14-17 and 18-20 (so Diamond) nor 11-12, 13, 14-16, 17 and 18-20 (so O'Connor), but 11-12, 13-15, 16-17 and 18-20.

Given these four units, it is possible to isolate one principle involved in the patterning of material in chapters 11-20 including the laments. The basic arrangement of material within each of the four units includes three elements: a superscription; a prophetic story designed to indict the people; and a prophetic lament. This basic pattern of which the laments are a part suggests a function for the laments besides their earlier purpose of defending Jeremiah's prophetic legitimacy. Instead of defending Jeremiah's prophetic ministry, the laments in context function to illustrate the guilt of the people, pointing to the necessity of the exile, as Diamond (1987:56) and O'Connor (1988:158) have observed. The linkage between the introductory story and the laments is provided by the references to the enemies in the laments. At the redactional level, the adversaries of the laments are implicitly understood to refer to those mentioned in the introductory prophetic story. While the evidence does not permit the conclusion that the pattern of prophetic story plus prophetic lament represented one redactional stage in the development of chapters 11-20, this possibility may be mentioned.

Chapter Three addresses the material within chapters 11-20 besides the introductory prophetic stories and the laments. This remaining material consists mostly of divine speeches which function in a variety of ways. The divine speeches highlight the relationship between Yahweh and Jeremiah, a point often made in discussions of the laments (e.g., von Rad 1983; Polk 1984; Fretheim 1987). The basis for the depiction of this relationship was explicit already in what may have existed in an earlier stage of tradition, namely in the divine responses to the laments. The divine speeches standing between the introductory prophetic story and the prophetic laments highlight the relationship between Yahweh and Jeremiah even more than the divine answers to the laments, and they serve as a further defense of Jeremiah's prophetic ministry.

The laments in context partake of three additional purposes beyond the laments' original function of defending the legitimacy of Jeremiah's prophetic vocation in the face of resistance. The laments in context function to announce Yahweh's judgement against Israel, to show the people's fault and the impact of that sin on Yahweh as the spurned partner to the covenant, and finally, to present Jeremiah's special identification with Yahweh as sign and symbol of Israel's relationship with Yahweh. In sum, the laments in context are designed primarily to present the guilt of the people and the necessity of judgement, themes which Diamond (1987:183) offers as the larger purpose of chapters 11-20. The goal of the laments in both their original usage and their redacted contexts is not a sensitive appreciation of the prophet. Diamond (1987:63, 158, 161, 170) also notes that the framework for the present form of chapters 11-20 is dialogic in character; this observation is noted in detail in Chapter Three. Connections between various units, not only the laments and their immediate contexts, are offered in this chapter. As a result of approaching the laments from the perspective of their contexts, the laments do not assume a role larger than what the contexts would indicate. The pain of Jeremiah expressed in the laments is not the ultimate message of the book; rather, it constitutes one eloquent part of chapters 11-20.

Chapter Four offers a few remarks on the contexts of the laments by examining how chapters 11-20 fit into their larger context, generally agreed to constitute chapters 7-25 (Thiel 1973, 1983; O'Connor 1989:617-18, 627, 630). Some themes in chapters 7-10 continue into chapters 11-20, though with some significant changes. These thematic variations affect the interpretation of the laments and their contexts. More precisely, the changes dramatize the guilt of Jeremiah's enemies and the prophet's inability to help them. The laments in their contexts in chapters 11-20 serve an important function in relation to chapters 21-25 as well. Chapters 11-20 establish the guilt of Jeremiah's unnamed adversaries whose identity is fully unveiled in chapters 21-25.

The social science format for citations has been adopted in order to reduce the number of footnotes and therefore the amount of time diverted from the main argument of this essay. Explanations for most decisions in translation are apparent from the footnotes to the translations. Otherwise, recourse to three recent commentaries on Jeremiah (Carroll 1986; Holladay 1986; McKane 1986) will indicate the underlying basis for translations; these three studies have facilitated this research in many ways. In translations, an attempt to follow the word order of Hebrew texts has been made, as long as it did not completely ruin the English rendering (cf. Holladay 1986:xii). The first letter of every word beginning a line is capitalized for the sake of convention. Smoother, and sometimes more poetic, translations can be found in either the NAB or NJPS translations. In conformity with the relative line-length of the Hebrew, translations are compact, relative to most available translations. Both verbs and the direct objects of the same root ("cognate accusatives") which these verbs govern, are rendered in translation by the same English root.

ONE

❧❧

The Laments of Jeremiah

The book of Isaiah presents the words of Yahweh, oracle after oracle. There is relatively little description of the prophet, Isaiah, except in his vision of Yahweh in chapter 6 and the biographical episodes of chapters 36-39. The book of Ezekiel contains more material about the prophet, mostly in the form of his symbolic actions. These episodes reflect little on the person of Ezekiel, however, since they are designed to point to the divine will. The book of Jeremiah presents the figure of the prophet in a very different way. Unlike any other prophetic work, the book of Jeremiah concentrates dramatically on the figure of the prophet himself. No other prophetic book devotes such a high percentage of material to descriptions of the prophet's life. Here, unlike any other prophet, Jeremiah is drawn emotionally before the audience in an intimate portrait. It is precisely this attention to the prophet and his dialogue with Yahweh that serves as vehicle for the divine message of the book.

At the core of the portrait of the prophet are the "laments," or as they are sometimes called, the "complaints" of the prophet, contained in Jer 11:18-23, 12:1-6, 15:15-21, 17:14-18, 18:18-23 and 20:7-13. The laments resemble individual laments in the psalms, but the prophetic laments reflect individual stylizing; they were not simply borrowed from the cult (Baumgartner 1988:45-46, 51, 54, 59, 62, 70, 74-76, 80-82, 89-92, 101; Holladay 1986:360). According to Baumgartner, distinctive prophetic features include the warning in 11:18, the divine word with introduction in 11:21-23, the reproach in 15:18b, the abrupt opening of 18:18, the content of 20:7a, 9a, and the aim to denounce in 20:11.

The laments share a number of features. Each lament is unique in the way it uses these elements, plays on them, reverses them. Five elements generally common to the laments are: (1) a prophetic invocation of God; (2) a direct speech of the enemies of Jeremiah (G.V. Smith 1979:230); (3) the prophet's declaration of his own innocence; and (4) the prophet's request for vengeance against his enemies. The placement of these elements in the laments, in addition to an occasional fifth element, the divine answer to the prayer of the prophet, may be illustrated in the following schema:

Laments No.:	I	II	III	IV	V	VI
Invocation/ Mention of God	11:18	12:1	15:15	17:14	18:19	20:7
Speech of Enemies	11:19	12:1c-2	—	17:15	18:20a (cf. 18)	20:10
Declaration of Innocence	11:19	12:3	15:16-18	17:16	18:20b	20:7
Request for Vengeance	11:20	12:3b-4	15:15	17:18	18:21-22a	20:11-12
Divine Answer to Prayer (?)	11:21-23	12:5-6	15:19-21	cf. 17:19f.	cf. 19:1f.	cf. 20:13

It may be noted that the arrangement of the laments is secondary. The final element, the divine answer, appears to be secondary by and large. This is evident from the lack of a divine answer in some laments (17:19f.; 19:1f.) and from the prose nature of other divine answers (11:21-23; 19:1f.). Still other divine responses (12:5-6; 15:19-21; 20:13) are questionable on other grounds (see below).

Two units sometimes included among the laments, namely 15:10-15 and 20:14-18, have been omitted from consideration in this chapter. These two units differ form-critically from the other prophetic soliloquies (Baumgartner 1988:73, 77; O'Connor 1988:76-78; cf. Diamond 1989:695). They constitute a different type of unit from the lament, namely the curse; these units bear little formal similarity to the laments. There is no calling upon Yahweh, no reference to enemies, no quotation of their words, no declaration of personal innocence, no request for divine vengeance, no answer from Yahweh. According to Holladay (1986:36), there are also poetic grounds for separating the second curse from the laments. Jer 11:20 and 20:12 repeat, forming an envelope around the material within. Holladay concludes that since 20:14-18 follows the end of the envelope, this unit stands outside the material contained inside the envelope structure, which includes the prophet's laments.

1. JEREMIAH 11:18-23

The first lament stands out from the preceding prose unit by virtue of its poetic form. The first lament has three verses:

(18)   Yahweh informed me and I knew;
        Then you showed me their deeds.
(19)   And I like a tame lamb was led to the slaughter;
        And I did not know that against me they schemed schemes:
        "Let us destroy the tree in its strength,
        And let us sever him from the land of the living,
        That his name be remembered no more."
(20)   O Yahweh of hosts, who judges righteously,
        Who tries the heart and the mind,
        Let me see your vengeance upon them,
        For to you I have revealed my case.

Notes to 11:18-20
The initial position of the expression "against me" in v 19 is emphatic (for other examples, see Muraoka 1985:43). Following NJPS, literally "kidneys" and "heart" are translated as "heart" and "mind" in v 20. According to Wolff (1974:65-66), the kidneys are the seat of the conscience. Yahweh is called the one who tests the heart and kidneys in Pss 7:9; 26:2; Jer 11:20; 17:10; 20:12. For a critique of this reification of linguistic terms for body parts to represent human qualities, see Lauha 1983. For further discussion of the role of "heart" and similar personal terms in Jeremiah, see Polk 1984:35-57. V 19c perhaps evokes associations tied to family inheritance (see Bloch-Smith 1990); this would include the proper familial commemoration (*zkr*; see note 4 below) and continuation of the family on the ancestral land.

The first line does not stress what Yahweh made the prophet know; the content is delayed for a line. Rather, the emphasis initially falls on the point that Yahweh made Jeremiah know. The line does not provide the audience with specific information, but relates how Yahweh drove knowledge into the prophet: "Yahweh made it known to me and I knew." Yahweh is the agent of knowing, and the result is Jeremiah, the knowing prophet. The first verb is active and causative; the second communicates a condition or state (Held 1965:272-82). The double use of the verb "to know" (*ydᶜ) and the shift in the subject of the verbs from Yahweh as agent to Jeremiah as recipient dramatizes the connectedness of Yahweh's causing to know and Jeremiah's knowing; it also evokes the personal force of this knowledge.

The knowledge is one of the whole person and it involves more than a transfer of information. Jeremiah sees the evil deeds of his enemies, who up to this point remain unnamed. The lack of an antecedent for the pronominal suffix in "their deeds" indicates the secondary nature of the present context of the passage (McKane 1986:254-55), a fact also casting some doubt on the supposition that the laments stand in chronological order, as argued by O'Connor (1988:157; cf. Overholt 1988:619). The evil deeds of these unnamed figures concern the prophet; these are not simply sins against God or humanity in general. Verse 19 spells out this point: "I was like a gentle lamb led to the slaughter. I did not know (*ydᶜ) it was against me they devised schemes..." The sins are directed against the life of the prophet; he did not *know*. He "was like a gentle lamb," a line paralleled in the fourth Suffering Servant Song (Isa 53:7). Indeed, it has been argued that the passage in Second Isaiah is dependent on the portrait of Jeremiah (Paul 1969). The theme of the enemies, however personally threatening, is general in its formulation. The enemies remain unnamed; their relationship to Jeremiah is as of yet unknown.

In v 19, the words of the unnamed enemies are quoted, and the themes of the prophetic ministry are evoked. The tree is Jeremiah, and his prophetic word is the fruit. The enemies express the wish to deny him a name in Israel, a high value; as is said in Eccles 7:1: *ṭôb šēm miššemen ṭôb*, "a good name is better than good oil." In v 20 Jeremiah appeals to the justice of God. Like many individual laments, the prophet pleads his innocence and appeals to Yahweh for divine justice, as Yahweh is the one who "tries the heart." The prophet closes his appeal with the sentiment that he has placed his fate in God's hands.

The divine answer that follows in 11:21-23 is apparently prosaic in form:

(21)   Therefore thus says Yahweh concerning the men of
         Anathoth,
         Those who seek your life, saying:
         "You shall not prophecy in the name of Yahweh

And you will not die by our hand."

(22) Therefore thus says Yahweh of hosts:
"See, I am about to bring judgement upon them,
The choice will die by the sword,
Their sons and their daughters will die by famine.

(23) And they will have no remainder
Because I will bring evil on the men of Anathoth
In the year of their visitation.

Notes to 11:21-23

LXX omits *lkn...ṣbʾt* in 11:22. According to Janzen (1973:85), the repetition of the introduction is out of place. It has been claimed that 11:21-23 is prose (e.g., Diamond 1987:23); McKane (1986:254) states that the only poetic material in 11:18-23 is v 20. In contrast, the preceding unit is usually taken as poetry; hence, it has been argued that the two pieces are unrelated. This view of matters assumes a rather distinct line between the poetry and prose in this book. Hubmann (1978:60-74) reads the lines in 11:18-23 (with the exception of 11:21) as poetry: v 21 scans as 4/3 (bracketing the prose introduction), v 22 as 3/3/4 (bracketing the prose introduction), and v 23 as 4/4 (bracketing the addition of "men of Anathoth"). (Even in these lines, the "additions" might be viewed as features of the "poetic-prose" found elsewhere in Jeremianic material.) The line-length and parallelism of the terms in 11:21-23, two hallmarks of biblical poetry, differ little from some passages which McKane interprets as poetry. While the distinction between poetry and prose in the Bible has been a matter of particular debate (see Cooper 1987; Diamond 1987:28, 135, 245 n. 6), the question is especially difficult in the book of Jeremiah. Jeremiah stands between the more concise poetry of the eighth century prophets and the longer length of lines of later prophets such as Joel.

The function of this unit is to make a concrete identification of the enemies named in the laments (McKane 1986:255). While divine answers are attested for laments (e.g., Pss 12:6; 60:8-10; 108:8-10), there are reasons for believing that this one is secondary in character. These would include, besides its prosaic character, the intrusion of the "men of Anathoth" and the two uses of *lākēn*, "therefore," without introduction or reason.

Perhaps the language in vv 21-23 was modeled on the lament itself. Indeed, superficial coherence between the lament and the "divine response" is provided through the following common items: *yhwh ṣĕbāʾôt* (11:20, 22); *šēm* (11:19, 21); *ʿal* (11:18, 21); **pqd* (11:20, 23); *lōʾ* (11:19, 21, 23); *kî* (11:19, 23); and perhaps alliteration between *rîbî* and *rāʿāb* (11:20, 22).

Furthermore, there is only superficial coherencè within vv 21-23; the only coherence of form resides in the use of *lākēn* clauses, the use of the root **mwt* and the two references to "the men of Anathoth." Unlike any other material within the prophetic laments (Wilson 1980:245), this divine response specifically names Jeremiah's enemies, the "men of Anathoth," his hometown, according to Jer 1:1 and 32:6-8. Morover, Yahweh's speech quotes these enemies as denying Jeremiah his prophetic mission: "Do not prophesy in the name of Yahweh, or you will die by our hand." Yahweh then announces his plan to punish them, to destroy every last one of them. It has been argued that the reference to "the men of Anathoth" in the divine response is intrusive (Hubmann 1978:169-72; Holladay 1986:364, 369-71; O'Connor 1988:18). Holladay (1986:371) suggests that the intrusion was inspired by the reference to Jeremiah's "brothers" and "father" in 12:6, the mention of his "mother" in 14:1 and 15:9, and the allusion to both parents in 20:14-18. ("My familiar friends," *ʾĕnôš šĕlōmî*, in 20:10 might be included in this list.) The addition, "the men of Anathoth," would then postdate the juxtaposition of the first two laments; in any case, the conspicuously longer length of this final line seems to reflect its secondary character. If this reading of the addition is correct, it would indicate that the laments originally had no specifically named enemies; the naming of names belongs to the redaction of the material. A further reason for suspecting that the divine answer postdates the positioning of the first lament with the second would be the links between the two laments, as the following discussion indicates.

2. JEREMIAH 12:1-6

The second lament follows on the heels of the first, and it gives the appearance of a continuing dialogue between the prophet and the deity (Holladay 1986:365; cf. O'Connor 1988:16-18), although the juxtaposition is secondary (Baumgartner 1988:70-71; McKane 1986:253-55; Overholt 1988:617):

(1)   Righteous are you, O Yahweh;
        When I complain to you,
        Yet I would litigate with you:
(2)   Why does the way of the wicked prosper?

Why do all who are treacherous thrive?
You plant them, they also take root;
They grow, they also produce fruit;
Near you are in their mouth
But far from their heart.

(3)   And you, Yahweh, you know me;
        You see me, and you test (how) my heart (is) with you
        Pull them out like sheep for the slaughter,
        And set them apart for the day of killing.
(4)   How long will the land mourn,
        And the grass of every field wither?
        For the wickedness of those who dwell in it,
        The beasts and the birds are swept away,
        Because they said, "He will not see our final lot."

Notes to 12:1-4
The *kî* clause in 12:1 is perhaps dependent on the following clause, not the preceding (see McKane 1986:260); otherwise, translations perhaps should reflect the point of Aejmelaeus (1986) that *kî* clauses that follow the main verb are causal in force. For **dbr mšpṭm ʾt*, "to litigate with" in 12:1, see BDB 1048; cf. Holladay 1986:376. The expression *ûbāḥantā libbî ʾittāk* consists of two clauses, the main verb of perception **bḥn*, plus the dependent nominal clause *libbî ʾittāk* (cf. Judg 16:15: *wĕlibbĕkā ʾên ʾittî*, "but your heart is not with me"; cf. Jer 15:20: *kî-ʾittĕkā ʾănî*, "for I am with you"); see also the analogous example in Gen 40:14 [cited in Holladay 1986:378]: *zĕkartanî ʾittĕkā*, "remember how I was with you...". For the lack of concord in number and gender between *bĕhēmôt* and *sāpĕtâ* in v 4, see Joüon 150g. For the sense of *ʾaḥărîtēnû* in v 4, cf. Ps 73:17 (see Diamond 1987:215 n. 67).

The legal metaphor of "case" (**rîb*) begins with the description of Yahweh as "righteous," and immediately gives this lament a legal cast. This word represents an opening statement of Jeremiah, the prosecuting attorney. The defendant, Yahweh, is innocent, but there are fundamental questions of theodicy, of evil in a world created and maintained by Yahweh the "righteous" (Baumgartner 1988:65). Unlike the so-called wisdom theology that the evil do not fare well in the world, i.e. "take root" (see Psalm 1; Koch 1983), in fact to Jeremiah's eyes, they are prospering (v 2). These evil ones are all the more insulting to Yahweh's prophet since they have Yahweh's name in their mouths, but nowhere else; the thought of Yahweh is far from their lives and selves, signalled by "their heart."

Jeremiah contrasts the enemies' situation with his own condition. He is innocent in the eyes of God (v 3). On the basis of his innocence and the evildoers' wickedness, Jeremiah calls for their slaughter instead of his own, discussed in the first lament (11:19). The expression of this wish with the verb *qdš perhaps puns implicitly on the description of enemies in v 3b; their unholy condition described in v 3b leads to their separation, *qdš, for sacrifice. This call is followed in v 4 by a classic lament question of "how long?" (cf. Ps 74:10). The lament then describes the effects of wickedness in the land: evil destroys it. Unlike the wicked who seem to be bearing fruit, the land languishes. Here there is a basic conceptual relationship between creation and humanity, between fruitfulness and sin. Creation participates in the divine order, which humanity can throw into chaos through its sin. As the final clause of v 4 suggests, the lamentable state of the land is attributed to wicked men who deny divine agency in the world and hence the divinely ordered relationships between Yahweh, humanity and creation.

The relationship between the first two laments is poignant. Together the two laments present to the audience the special relationships among Yahweh, Jeremiah and the wicked. Specifically, there are four thematic points of contact between the two laments. First, knowledge forms the keynote theme of the first lament and resurfaces as a theme in the second lament. In the first lament, knowledge is a question of Jeremiah's personal fate from the perspective of threatening enemies. In the second lament, knowledge works on a fundamental level upon which all else hangs, including the prophet's personal fate. This is Yahweh's knowledge of the personal depths of Jeremiah. This sets the stage for a basic point in the second lament: the defense of Jeremiah's prophetic legitimacy in terms of theodicy. The second lament utilizes the theme of theodicy to address the prophet's situation (cf. Stulman 1989:318).

Second, the images of growth and the land appear in both laments. In the first lament, the enemies call for the destruction of "the tree," Jeremiah himself, and "its strength," his word (11:19). The enemies declare that the prophet should be cut off from "the land of the living," namely this world (cf. Ps 27:13). In the second lament, Jeremiah describes the success of evil as planted and bringing forth fruit; then he laments the condition of the world rendered desolate due to its evil (12:2a, 4a). Which plant will be cut off? And what result will this produce? This gulf between Jeremiah, on the one hand, and the enemies, on the other hand, is recapitulated on the structural level. Both laments devote an initial comment to the wicked (11:18b, 19b; 12:1b-2) and then contrast the innocence of the prophet (11:20; 12:3). This contrast is reinforced with the word, "but," which introduces both descriptions of Jeremiah's innocence in 11:20 and 12:3. There is a chasm between Jeremiah and his enemies expressed by their rhetorical separation and the contrasting "but." The structure is reminiscent of Psalm 1 which also contrasts the ways of the wicked and the righteous. Holladay (1986:376-377) suspects that Jeremiah is playing off this psalm. Theodicy as Jeremiah expresses it in 12:1 is posed in a way similar to wisdom texts such as Psalm 73 and Job 21.

Third, the second lament continues the image of Yahweh as one who "tries the heart and mind" (*bōḥēn kĕlāyôt wālēb*) (11:20; 12:3; cf. 12:2). The formulaic phrase, *kĕlāyôt wālēb*, in the first lament appears as a word-pair in the second (Avishur 1984:592-93; on this technique, see Melamed 1961). The first lament ends with this image of Yahweh. In the first lament, it is stated as a general title of Yahweh, but in the second lament, the basic principle inherent in the title is pushed to its logical and personal conclusions. Yahweh is not simply the one who "tries the heart"; Yahweh tries the heart of the prophet, and this is the basis for further discussion. Here the root *rʾh* plays a part in linking the two laments; the alliteration of consonants /r/ and /ʿ/ and /r/ and /ʾ/ perhaps reinforces the sense of evil in both laments. The clustering of /r/, /ʿ/ and /ʾ/ in the first lament is weak: *hôdîʿanî wāʾēdāʿâ...hirʾîtanî* (v 18); *wĕlōʾyādaʿtî* (v 19); *ʾerʾeh* (v 20); *rāʿāb* (v 22); *rāʿâ* (v 23). In the second lament, the consonance formed by these sounds is resounding. The patterning of /r/, /ʿ/ and /ʾ/ includes *ʾārîb...ʾădabbēr...rĕšāʿîm* (12:1), *tirʾēnî* (12:3), *hāʾāreṣ...mērāʿat...ʾāmĕrû...yirʾeh...ʾaḥărîtēnû* (12:4). In 11:18, Yahweh has shown Jeremiah the evil of his enemies although in 12:4 they express their belief that Yahweh does not see their destiny (see also wordplay on *ʾḥr* in 11:19 and 12:4; *ṣdq* in 11:20 and 12:1).

Finally, the second lament reverses the image of the sheep as victim. In the first lament, the enemies identify Jeremiah as the victim, and in his second lament, Jeremiah applies this image to his adversaries.

The answer from Yahweh in verse 5 does not resolve the tension. Rather, Yahweh allows Jeremiah and his enemies to remain in competition:

(5)   If you raced on foot and they wearied you,
       Then how will you compete with horses?

And if in a safe land you fall,

How will you do in the jungle of the Jordan?

(6)   For even your brothers, indeed your father's house,

Even they, they have dealt treacherously with you,

Even they, they address you constantly;

Do not believe them

Because they tell you good things.

Notes to 12:5-6

The *kî* of v 5a extends also to the question of v 5c, as the parallel structures of the protases and apodoses indicate. For the two uses of *kî* in this verse, see Aejmelaeus 1986. On *bōṭēaḥ* as "fall" on the basis of Arabic **bṭḥ*, see Kopf 1958:165-68; Ehrman 1960:153-55; *HALAT* (third edition) 116; McKane 1986: 263-64. Bright (1965:87) and O'Connor (1988:11) criticize this view. The cognate is philologically feasible (McKane 1986:264). The idea is as well; it provides a great suggestion of trust, an issue taken up in the concluding words of the same verse, "do not believe them." Holladay (1986:380) rejects Arabic **bṭḥ* as cognate since the first stem of Arabic **bṭḥ* is transitive; this objection is inconclusive. Holladay instead offers this interpretation: "If it takes a land without drought for you to exhibit trust (in me), then what will you do in the thicket of the Jordan?" The thrust of such an analogy is unclear. According to O'Connor, the simpler sense of BH **bṭḥ*, "to trust," could suit the context. O'Connor (1988:11) states: "what is at stake is Jeremiah's lack of preparation for adversity. If he cannot manage in a safe land, how will he deal with the increasing peril ahead?" This interpretation could suit the second meaning of **bṭḥ* as well, however. There are two reasons for accepting **bṭḥ*, "to fall," in Jer 12:5. First, Kopf (1958:165-68) notes a number of passages which juxtapose **bṭḥ* with **škb* (e.g., Job 11:18) and **rbṣ* (2 Kgs 18:21//Isa 36:6; cf. Isa 14:30; Hos 2:20). Second, **bṭḥ* with the preposition *b-* rarely applies, if ever, to places; rather, it is used of people (including Yahweh) and their personal qualities. In contrast **bṭḥ ʿl* is predicated of places. For the unsupported emendation of *bigʾôn hayyardēn* to *gê hayyardēn* in v 5, see Winckler 1895:292 (is the unusual expression *bigʾôn hayyardēn* related to the similar expressions in 13:8?).

Diamond (1987:49) notes contexts (1 Sam 20:37, 38; 24:9) where **qrʾ ʾḥr* serves "to introduce direct speech to the person concerned." The word *mālēʾ* is presumed to be adverbial, modifying the verb rather than part of direct speech (cf. Diamond 1987:37). Diamond (1987:49) gives a meaning of "assemble" for **mlʾ* in this context and cites *qirʾû malʾû* in Jer 4:5 as support; the meaning is unconvincing. Furthermore, the citation of Jer 4:5, *qirʾû malʾû*, though parallel, is not to be taken as meaning "assemble! help!" (so Diamond); rather, *malʾû* may constitute hendiadys with *qirʾû* and modify it adverbially (so McKane 1986:90: "give this message the fullest publicity").

Hence two idioms underlie *qārĕ'û 'aḥărêkā mālē'* in Jer 12:6, namely **qr' 'ḥr* and **qr'* plus **ml'*. The emphatic use of the independent pronouns is replicated in translation. For the emphatic use of the independent pronoun in v 3, see Muraoka 1985:53 (for another use of independent pronouns to express emphasis, see the remarks on Jer 17:18). For *gam* before the personal pronoun in v 6 for emphasis, see MacDonald 1975:166 n. 13.

This divine response offers little consolation. Rather, it leaves Jeremiah to fend off his enemies and their conspiracies against him. The words, * *'ereṣ* in 12:5, 6, and *'aḥărîtēnû* in v 4 and *'aḥărêkā* in v 6 loosely connect the divine response of 12:5-6 to 12:1-4. McKane (1986:287) rejects v 5 as part of the divine response and assigns it to part of the prophetic speech on the basis of its unparalleled topic; the reason is unconvincing. The common root **dbr* in vv 1 and 6 encases the six verses.

This response bears so many verbal resemblances with the lament that it might be argued that the response was built out of the vocabulary of the lament. Verbal roots in common are: **bgd* (12:1, 6); **'ḥr* (12:4, 6); **dbr* (12:1, 6); *'rṣ* (12:4, 5). A number of particles in the lament reappear in the response: **'el* (12:1, 6); *'et* (12:4, 5 [two times]; *gam* (12:2, 6 [three times]); *kî* (12:1, 4, 5, 6 [two times]). In other words, sixteen of the thirty-eight words (not including proclitics and enclitics) in the response also appear in the lament proper. Some verbal echoes repeat as well: *šālû* in 12:1 / / *šālôm* in 12:5; **ṭbḥ* in 12:3 / /**bṭḥ* in 12:5; *'ak* in 12:1 / /*'êk* in 12:5.

The two laments portray Yahweh's prophetic servant, Jeremiah, in pain and fear. Yet, the mood and tone of this servant differ from the posture of the Suffering Servant of Second Isaiah, as Holladay (1986:360) notes. Jeremiah is no Suffering Servant in the sense that he is meek; he subjects Yahweh to questioning. He prays for vengeance (Jer 11:20 = 20:12; 15:15) and he calls for the death of parts of the Judean population (Jer 11:22; cf. 18:21-22a).

3. JEREMIAH 15:15-21

The third lament moves away from judicial metaphor and claims of innocence found in the first two laments. Instead, it baldly states Jeremiah's call for revenge:

(15)   You, you know, Yahweh
         Remember me and visit me,

And avenge yourself for me upon my persecutors.

Do not in your anger take me away;

Know that I bear reproach because of you.

(16)   Your words were found, and I ate them.

And your words were joy to me

And the delight of my heart;

For your name is called upon me,

O Yahweh, God of hosts.

(17)   I did not sit in the company of merrymakers;

Nor did I rejoice;

Because of your hand, alone I sat,

For you filled me with indignation.

(18)   Why is my pain unceasing,

My wound uncurable,

Unsusceptible to healing?

You are like a deceitful brook to me,

Like waters that fail.

Notes to 15:15-18

For *nqm, "avenge oneself" in the Niphal plus *mn* for adversaries and *l-* for whose behalf in v 15, see *BDB* 668; Baumgartner 1988:47-48. Holladay (1986:457) renders *nqm as "to exercise sovereignty," but against Mendenhall (1973:97) whom Holladay cites as the basis for this interpretation of this root, see Pitard 1982. For *nṣ³ ḥrph ʿl, "bear reproach for" in v 15, see also Ps 69:8; Zeph 3:18 (*BDB* 357). For the textual issues underlying yhwh ³lhy ṣb³t in v 16, see Janzen 1973:79-80. "Your hand" is an expression in v 17 for "because of Yahweh." For bādād yāšabtî in v 17, cf. Lam 1:1: yāšĕbâ bādād, "she sits lonely" (also Lam 3:28; Lev 13:46; see Holladay 1986:460). For niqrā³ šem yhwh ʿal in v 16 for divine ownership, see *BDB* 896, citing also Deut 28:10; 2 Sam 6:2 = 1 Chron 13:6; Isa 63:19; Jer 14:9; Amos 9:12; 2 Chron 7:14. Galling (1956) argued that this expression had a secular basis in legal transactions of property in which new owners used to call out their name over the property. Carroll (1986:330) and Holladay (1986:246) also understand the expression as one of ownership; the view is old (e.g., Budde 1899:197). In this case it means that Yahweh's name is "attached" (NJPS) to Jeremiah. The final bicolon has been interpreted as a question (RSV; Carroll 1986:329). In contrast, Baumgartner (1988:50), Holladay (1986:451) and McKane (1986:350) view it as a statement, and NAB and NJPS translate the bicolon as a declarative statement. Although a question need not be marked explicitly by the interrogative hê in direct discourse (see Joüon 137p), there is no compelling reason to view this instance as a question.

In both style and theme, the third lament initially recalls the first two laments. The lament opens with an especially strong invocation of Yahweh and an expression of the divine knowledge, a theme voiced in the first two laments. In this lament, divine knowledge is concomitant with divine action, and here Jeremiah calls for revenge. At this point the third lament moves away from the style of the first two laments. Unlike them, the third lament neither describes nor quotes the evil men (G. V. Smith 1979). It abbreviates the description of enemies versus Jeremiah. Rather, it calls directly for revenge for the enemies and vindication for Jeremiah. The particle ʾal is separated from the verb which it negates. The other cases of this phenomenon noted by Joüon (160g), Pss 6:2, 38:2 and Isa 64:8, also appear in prayers. Joüon regards this word-order as an instance of emphasis; it appears especially appropriate to contrast the prophet's request for himself with his wishes directed against his enemies.

The basis for the prophet's call for revenge is his relationship with Yahweh. V 16 begins a recapitulation of Jeremiah's ministry on behalf of Yahweh. The prophet recalls his initial encounter with the divine word, how he found these words and how he ate them. The style of this sentence is reminiscent of the opening of the first lament, but it reverses the active divine voice and the passive prophetic voice. The passive expression, "your words were found," starts psychologically with Yahweh; these words are Yahweh's words. The sentence ends in the active expression of Jeremiah's action, "and I ate them." Here Jeremiah stands in the bloom of his prophetic vocation. His eating of the words echoes Yahweh's putting the divine words to Jeremiah's mouth in chapter 1 (v 9). According to the third lament, the divine words were joy and delight to the prophet (Jer 15:16), and here there is a reversal of the opening verse of this lament. Whereas now pain is the result of being Yahweh's prophet, originally joy and delight marked the prophetic vocation. This verse contrasts less the enemies and the prophet, and more the initial and current states of Jeremiah's status as prophet, since as the prophet says in v 16, he is called by the name of Yahweh, God of hosts.

What does this identification mean now for the prophet? V 17 describes the implications of being called by the name of Yahweh. The verse contrasts the prophet's behavior with the general norms of his society. He sits alone, apart from the social activities of the people. The reason given for this state of the prophet's life is that Yahweh has filled Jeremiah with divine indignation (cf. 6:11). The disposition of the deity and the prophet toward the people is not merely the same; the prophet's posture derives from Yahweh. Like the word from Yahweh, the divine anger now fills the prophet; Jeremiah feels what Yahweh feels toward Israel. While v 17 is a daring expression of the relationship between Yahweh and Jeremiah, it does not resolve the tension involved in this relationship. Although he is Yahweh's prophet, Jeremiah is still not rescued. His pain is unceasing. And this pain names Yahweh as its cause; Yahweh could fulfill Jeremiah's requests and resolve the problem. Yet the prophet sees that Yahweh has not done so. V 18 is reproachful in its question to Yahweh. With his question Jeremiah removes the presumption of divine goodwill. The irony expressed in the metaphor of this final question is captured by the polyvalent quality of the image, and that is the notion that Jeremiah needs the waters who are Yahweh (cf. Ps 42:1-2). Water is physically necessary for human life; it is a requirement for living things including humanity. So also Yahweh; Yahweh is necessary for human life, and without Yahweh, humanity withers and dies. Jeremiah needs these waters despite their apparent unreliability.

The divine response in vv 19-20 is conditional, challenging Jeremiah's claims regarding himself:

(19)   Therefore thus says Yahweh:
         "If you return, I will restore you,
         Before me you shall stand;
         If you utter what is precious,
         Rather than what is worthless,
         As my mouth you shall be.
         They, they shall turn to you,
         But you, you shall not turn to them.

(20)   And I will make you for this people
         Into a fortified bronze wall;
         They will fight against you,
         But they shall not prevail over you,
         For I am with you
         To save you and deliver you
         — Oracle of Yahweh —

(21)   I will deliver you out of the hand of the wicked,
         And redeem you from the grasp of the ruthless."

Yahweh neither accepts nor rejects Jeremiah's plea regarding his enemies; rather, the divine response returns the prophet to his prophetic
mission. In two conditional statements, Yahweh promises a special place
and role for the prophet. Placed in initial position for emphasis, the
phrases "before me" (*lĕpānay*) and "as my mouth" (*kĕpî*) indicate promise
for Jeremiah's future if he "returns" and "utters what is precious." Both
of these conditions refer to Jeremiah's continuing in his prophetic mission. This prophetic work will provoke, however, more opposition from
enemies. The last sentence of v 19 is ambiguous: the people shall return
to you, but you shall not return to them. Playing on the initial theme of
Jeremiah's turning to Yahweh, the divine response now shows that the
turning of the prophet means dealing with the turning of the people, i.e.
not repentance as "turning" often means in the book of Jeremiah, but
more opposition. For as v 20 conveys the point, Jeremiah will become yet
a city under siege, one that will ultimately survive, though not without
the pains of a besieged population. In the end of the third lament there is
Yahweh's assurance that "I am with you." Yet the race which Jeremiah
has to run is not finished. It is only at some future point that Yahweh will
finally rescue Jeremiah from the wicked (v 21).

4. JEREMIAH 17:14-18

The fourth lament does not engage the judicial metaphor presented
in the first two laments and abbreviated in the third lament. Jer 17:14-18
calls instead for the prophet's wholeness:

(14)   Heal me, Yahweh, that I may be healed;
         Save me that I may be saved;
         For you are my praise.
(15)   See them saying to me,
         "Where is the word of Yahweh?
         Let it come!"
(16)   But I, I did not hasten from being a shepherd after you,
         Nor the day of disaster have I desired
         You, you know the expression of my lips,
         It was ever before you.
(17)   Do not be a terror to me,
         My refuge you are on the evil day.

(18)   May my pursuers be shamed,
        But let me not be shamed;
        May they, they be dismayed,
        But may I, I not be dismayed;
        Bring upon them the evil day,
        And with double smashing smash them.

Notes to 17:14-18

The unconverted imperfect following the imperative in v 14a and a cohortative in v 14b may constitute a purpose or result clause (Joüon 116b, d; but see Joüon 114b, note 1; Meek 1955-56:40-43; Holladay 1986:505; cf. Orlinsky 1941-42:198). Kelly (1920:2, 14) classifies this instance as "being in the sphere of result." (I wish to thank S. E. Fassberg for this reference.) For the textual difficulties with MT *mērōʿeh* in v 16, see Barthélemy 1986:613-17; for various interpretations, see McKane 1986:410. McKane's view that MT reflects Yahweh as the shepherd is open to question, given the following prepositional phrase, *ʾaḥărēkā* (what would Yahweh's shepherding after himself mean?). The common emendation to **mērāʿâ*, "for evil", based on Aquila, Symmachus, and Syriac, is attractive in view of the parallel with "day of disaster" in the following line, but these versions apparently represent an attempt to render order from a difficult text. 4QJer[a] corresponds precisely to MT (Janzen 1973:178). MT (so also LXX) refers to Jeremiah's role as shepherd (so NJPS; Diamond 1987:79; Holladay 1986:505; Rashi and Kimchi apud McKane 1986:410). Holladay (1986:506) notes in v 17 the long imperfect (*tihyeh*) instead of the short form (*tĕhî*) with *ʾal*; for examples, see *GKC* 107p, 109a note 2; cf. 75hh. For *ʾal* with the cohortative in v 18, see Joüon 114c. The form *hābîʾ* in v 18 belongs to a group of Hiphil third ʾaleph imperative, jussive and converted imperfect forms with hireq or hireq yod instead of sere (Joüon 78i). Kesterson (1986:373) notes the high correspondence between these forms and their position before gutturals, ʾaleph, hê and ʿayin. The vowel before the ʾaleph in third ʾaleph verbs in these cases apparently removes from the middle position of sere to the back quality of the hireq due to the following guttural consonants; in short, a process of assimilation is involved.

Like the first lament, the fourth opens with an invocation of Yahweh and a double repetition of verbs in the first line. Here the prophet calls to Yahweh to heal so that he may be healed. The two verbs are integrally related; the first actively commands Yahweh's healing and the second passively communicates the hope for Jeremiah's healing. The second line of this lament replicates this structure in calling for "saving." Often this word-root **yšʿ* is translated "to save," or in its noun form, "salvation." This term may lack a certain concrete force in English, since as an impor-

tant theological term, it involves a spiritual relationship with God. That
dimension of the word is also at stake here, but for Jeremiah in this context it refers literally also to saving his life. The basis for these impera-
tives is stated in the last line of v 14: "you are my praise."

Verses 15-16 contrast the evildoers with Jeremiah in a rather striking
way, and it is this contrast which dominates the remainder of this lament. Vv 15-16 repeat for added emphasis the pronouns, "them," "I" and
"you." The repetition was grammatically unnecessary for BH, and the
three-fold repetition is especially conspicuous. The use of "I" versus
"them" is certainly designed to heighten the contrast between Jeremiah
and the enemies (Muraoka 1985:54-55), an antithesis drawn already in
the previous laments and repeated in verse 18. The evil press for the divine word, but not Jeremiah. The antithesis is set before Yahweh, "you,
you know." The phrase, "you, you know" (ʾattâ yādāʿtā) in v 16 is
"motivated by the desire to call special attention to the addressed"
(Muraoka 1985:53).

The phrase ʾattâ yādāʿtā also introduces an appeal based on Yahweh's
own divine nature and echoes the use of this same verb of knowing from
all three preceding laments. Yahweh knows. Vv 17-18 explicitly make
this appeal with a series of wishes (imperative and volitive forms). V 17
opens with the basic request, that Yahweh not be a terror to Jeremiah.
The Jeremiah filled with the indignation of Yahweh, and standing on the
side of Yahweh's word delivering it against opposition and threat to life
and limb, is the same Jeremiah who faces Yahweh as a threat.

The remainder of vv 17-18 dwells on the meaning of the request of
Yahweh not to be a terror. These verses ask that Jeremiah be saved from
his enemies and his enemies be destroyed. The requests are poetically
structured so that the "day of evil" stands at the beginning and the end
of the requests:

Verse 17:   A   refuge for Jeremiah on the "day of evil"
Verse 18:   B   request to put enemies to shame, but not Jeremiah
            B   request for enemies to be dismayed, but not Jeremiah
            A   destruction for enemies on the "day of evil"

The double use of the phrase "day of evil" forms an envelope (terms
marked "A") around the requests (terms marked "B"), and sets the tone
for them. What is to come is the day of evil or calamity for Israel. The
question of where the prophet and his foes will stand on that day presents an antithesis between Jeremiah and his opposition. Jeremiah seeks

the safety of Yahweh for himself and the destruction by Yahweh for his enemies. Underlying this series of requests is an implicit message about the enemies. In v 15 they are portrayed as asking for the word of Yahweh, and in v 18 this word comes in the form of destruction. The implicit message here is that the enemies have brought their own destruction upon themselves; they have literally asked for their own demise. In its present form, this lament has no divine response, unlike the preceding laments. What follows instead is a prose narrative commanding Jeremiah to speak to the people in Yahweh's name (v 20).

5. JEREMIAH 18:19-23

The fifth lament is preceded by a prose sentence describing the enemies' intentions towards the prophet (Jer 18:18):

Then they said, "Come and we will plot against Jeremiah, because law shall not perish from the priest, nor counsel from the wise, nor word from the prophet. Come and we will smite him with the tongue, and let us not heed any of his words."

Notes to 18:18
Imperative plus simple waw plus cohortative may indicate a purpose clause (see Joüon 116b; cf. Orlinsky 1940-41:376). Kelly (1920:14) takes the two verbs as coordinate. Kelly's view seems likely, as the command to "come" is not addressed to others with a purpose in mind; rather, the command represents self-addressed performative speech to go and do some action.

This passage opens in an irregular way insofar as there is no clear antecedent for "they." This sentence has been placed in this location for two reasons (see McKane 1986:lxvii). It introduces the fifth lament. By doing so, it continues the theme of enemies from the preceding lament and maintains the sense of threat to the hero, Jeremiah. Indeed, the contrast between enemies and Jeremiah has been a standard feature in the first, third and fourth laments. Furthermore, 18:18 gives a thematic context indicating the way in which the problem of prophecy in the waning days of the southern monarchy is to be understood. The speakers, the unnamed enemies, believe that the traditional roles of the priest, wise man and prophet continue as before, and that Jeremiah violates this tradition.

Indeed, this implicit tension is made explicit in Yahweh's command to
Jeremiah not to act as a traditional prophet in the role of mediator on behalf of the people. The verse is connected to the lament further through
the verbal link, *qšb, "to pay attention to" in vv 18 and 19.

With this context of evil fate lurking in the background, Jeremiah utters the words of the fifth lament (Jer 18:19-23):

(19)   Attend, Yahweh, to me,
        And listen to the voice of my adversaries:
(20)   "Should evil be paid for good?"
        For they have dug a pit for my life.
        Remember how I stood before you (*lĕpānêkā*),
        Speaking good for them,
        To turn back your fury from them.
(21)   Therefore give their children over to famine,
        And mow them down by the sword's edges.
        May their wives become childless widows.
        May their men be slain by Death,
        Their young men slain by the sword in battle.
(22)   May a cry be heard from their houses,
        Because you suddenly bring a marauder upon them (*ᶜălêhem*);
        For they have dug a pit to ensnare me,
        And traps they have hidden for my feet.
(23)   But you, Yahweh, you know
        All their deadly plans against me (*ᶜālay*).
        Do not pardon (*kpr*) their iniquity,
        And their sin from before you (*millĕpānêkā*) do not wipe out,
        And may they be made to stumble before you (*lĕpānêkā*),
        In the time of your anger act against them.

Notes to 18:19-23
For the textual and interpretational issues involving MT *yĕrîbay* in v 19, see
Barthélemy 1986:628-29; McKane 1986:438. This translation presumes that v
19b introduces the words of the adversaries quoted in v 20a (so Diamond
1987:88, 244 n. 2), in conformity with other speeches of enemies quoted in
other laments. The other possibility is to understand *yrby* as "case."
Barthélemy includes instances of *yĕrîb* as "case" rather than the more common "adversary." For the LXX of vv 20, 22, see Janzen 1973:27, 90. Diamond
(1987:249 n. 45) notes the inversion of the expected word order between the

subject and prepositional phrase; this syntax is perhaps designed to place
emphasis on "evil." Diamond rejects *rāʿâ* as the subject of the verb due to
the lack of gender agreement and instead construes the verb as an imper-
sonal passive with implicit personal agent. While there may be an implicit
personal agent underlying the clause (cf. 2 Sam 3:39), it does not suspend
the question of agreement between subject and predicate. Joüon 150j cites
passages where verbs preceding their feminine subjects do not agree in gender, including an example with *rāʿâ* (Isa 47:11). For qere *šyḥh* versus ketib
šwḥh, see McKane 1986:439; the root is **šḥḥ* and not **šwḥ* (so Held 1973:174-
81). The phrase *lammāwet* in v 23 is rendered adjectivally for concision. In v
23, the ketib is an imperfect, hence a jussive in accordance with the preceding requests; the qere is a converted perfect, stating the future condition of
the cursed.

The prose background of v 18 leads directly into the theme of the lament's opening verse. Indeed, v 18 becomes the referent for the enemies'
question in v 20. After calling on Yahweh by name and asking for divine
attention, Jeremiah raises the subject of how his enemies have treated
him. Rhetorically the prophet grounds his claim by quoting a question
that can only be answered negatively. He cites the enemies' asking if evil
is the correct payment for good, because it is precisely an evil fate which
the enemies have planned for him. The question recalls the question of
the second lament: "Why does the way of the wicked prosper?" (Jer
12:2). Here the setting of the question is turned on its head, because it is
precisely the evildoers who pose the question. Here the question bears a
more personal dimension than it has in the second lament. It involves directly the fate of the speakers. This question shall come back on them.
The question presumes that evil should not be the recompense for good,
but the implied referent of the question is misplaced. The enemies pose
the question, and therefore imply that they are in the right and the
prophet in the wrong. Yet they have it backwards: it is the prophet who
is good and the enemies who are evil to him, and the evil that they lament is the evil lying within themselves.

The lives of the enemies and the prophet are their most intertwined
in this lament. This lament premises the understanding of evil and good
for Jeremiah and the enemies on how each one functions in the mind of
the other. For the people, Jeremiah negates their understanding of
prophecy. His negative word violates their understanding of how the
prophetic word — and therefore Yahweh — are working in their world.
Jeremiah's life symbolizes what is wrong for them. Why is there is no assurance of peace from Jeremiah, like the peace announced by other
prophets (Jer 14:13)? For Jeremiah, the continuation of the unnamed en-

emies represents a questioning of his prophetic mission. Yahweh does not choose yet to exact a price for refusing the words of the prophet, which casts into doubt the veracity of Jeremiah's word. Rather, the enemies continue to plot against Jeremiah's life, provoking the prophet to seek the end of their life through a traditional means available to a prophet — seeking a divine response.

Jeremiah's statement of how he has served out his prophetic role of mediation before Yahweh forms the basis of his claim of innocence. Those for whom he gave his life now wish to destroy his life. Jeremiah stood before Yahweh and pleaded for the people; he sought to do good for them. Now Jeremiah stands before Yahweh and pleads for the people; this time it is to seek their wholesale destruction. Vv 21 and 22 recall the effects of war: famine, battle, widowhood, childlessness, pestilence personified in the figure of Death (cf. Jer 9:20; M. S. Smith 1987a), and perhaps pillage evoked by the description of a "marauder." Jeremiah asks for Death in vv 21-22, precisely because the people seek his death. In v 22b, they are described as typical evildoers seeking to trap the righteous (Prov 1:11).

When v 23 invokes Yahweh a second time, with the emphatic "you, you know," Jeremiah echoes the theme of divine knowledge from earlier laments. The verse also adds the point that Jeremiah's death is the goal of their plots. They desired death for Jeremiah (v 23); now he asks for their death (v 21). Earlier he turned away the wrath of Yahweh for them (v 20); now he asks for the divine anger for them (v 23). This contrast in vv 20 and 23 is highlighted further by the use of the preposition *ʿal: before Jeremiah spoke "for them," ʿălêhem (v 20b); now they act "against me," ʿālay (v 23a). This contrast is conveyed also through the use of *lipnê in the same verses: before he stood "*before you*" (lĕpānêkā), namely Yahweh, on the people's behalf (v 20), now he asks that their sin not be wiped out from *before* Yahweh (millĕpānêkā) and that they be made to stumble before Yahweh, "before you" (v 23). Rather than accept prophetic mediation as atonement before Yahweh, Jeremiah asks for the opposite, that Yahweh keep in mind their sin and act upon it in accordance with divine justice. The prophetic role here is not mediation for the people; it is judgement against them. This lament inverts the function of prophetic speech; the role of mediation is stood on its head. The laments are anti-prophetic in the sense that they violate the norms of prophetic speech. Indeed, this development within this lament comports with the suggestion of Seitz (1989a:10) concerning one function of the laments:

What is clear is that an avenue of discourse is cut off for the prophet. He can
no longer intercede on behalf of the people. This fact, and the restriction of
the prophetic word to judgement (20,8), gives rise to persecution and challenge on the horizontal plane. The loss of the intercessory role, in its social
dimension, gives rise to the intercessions of the prophet, as individual, on
his own behalf.

Seitz's comments are addressed to the redacted context of the laments,
and he notes other contexts where intercession is an issue in Jeremiah 11-
20 (11:14; 14:11; 15:1). Yet this view pertains also to this lament.

The inversion of prophetic speech signalling the impending judgement of the people is recapitulated within the structure of the lament as
well:

A invocation of Yahweh (v 19): "Yahweh..."
B the enemies dig a pit for Jeremiah (v 20a)
C the fate of the enemies (vv 21-22a)
B' the enemies dig a pit for Jeremiah (v 22b)
A' invocation of Yahweh (v 23): "Yahweh...you...your anger"

This envelope structure highlights the middle element, the fate of the enemies, and thereby hints at their ultimate destruction. The referent to the
question whether evil should be the payment for good is implicitly answered.

At the same time, the implicit resolution of the answer remains only
implicit; there is no real resolution for either party. From the audience's
perspective, the enemies remain alive, and Yahweh exacts no punishment yet against them. Jeremiah continues to escape with his life and
speaks, at least to the audience. The tension between Jeremiah and the
enemies who seek the end of each other's lives continues. Even
Jeremiah's final request leaves the tension open-ended to the future. He
requests that Yahweh act against the people in "the time of your anger."
It is a time that will surely come; but when? There is no divine response
following this lament. The "time of your anger" (v 23) remains unknown;
it is a future event. Furthermore, Jeremiah receives no answer from
Yahweh. The next section simply presents him commanded by God to
confront the people yet again.

6. JEREMIAH 20:7-13

The final lament brings to a close the court case between Yahweh and
Jeremiah:

(7)   You fooled me, Yahweh, and I was fooled;
        You seized me, and you prevailed (*ykl).
        I became a laughingstock all (kol) day;
        Everyone (kullōh) mocks me.

(8)   Whenever I speak, I cry out,
        "Lawlessness and destruction!" I call;
        For the word of Yahweh has become for me
        A reproach and derision all (kol) day.

(9)   If I say, "I will not mention him,
        And I will not speak anymore in his name,"
        It is in my heart like a burning fire,
        Shut up in my bones;
        And I have become wearied holding it in (kalkēl),
        And I cannot (*ykl).

(10)   For I hear many whispering,
        "Terror surrounding!"
        "Denounce him! Let us denounce him!"
        Say all (kōl) my familiar friends,
        Watching for my fall.
        "Perhaps he can be fooled
        And we could prevail (*ykl) over him,
        And take our revenge on him."

(11)   But Yahweh is with me like a strong warrior;
        Therefore my pursuers will stumble (*kšl),
        and will not prevail (*ykl).
        They will be greatly ashamed,
        For they will not succeed (*śkl),
        Their humiliation will never be forgotten.

(12)   O, Yahweh of Hosts, who tests the righteous,
        Examines the heart (kĕlāyôt) and the mind,
        May I see your revenge upon them,

For before you I have revealed my case.

(13)   Sing to Yahweh; praise Yahweh!
        For he has rescued the life of the needy
        From the hand of the evildoers.

Notes to Jer 20:7-13

According to Heschel (1962:113-14), the first line represents the seduction of
Jeremiah and the second line his rape. Less sexual interpretations are possible; see O'Connor 1988:70. Given the other images in the context, the sexual
interpretation seems unlikely (so Diamond 1987:110-11, 256 nn. 72-76). For
kullōh as "each one" in v 7, see Joüon 146j. While noting the textual problem,
Joüon 148a, note 1 includes *kĕʾēš bōʿeret ʿāsūr* in v 9 as one example of a masculine adjective following a feminine adjective modifying a feminine noun;
other examples appear in 1 Sam 15:9 and 1 Kgs 19:11. On **ykl* in v 9, see
Janzen 1973:31.

The sequence of tenses in the enemies' speech in v 10 is difficult. In v 10a,
haggîdû wĕnaggîdennû appears to be coordinate (Kelly 1920:14). For v. 10c
Joüon 116c speaks of the cohortative used in a "proposition optative," and
includes this passage in this paragraph, calling this particular example
"dubitative." The situation is a hypothetical one, marked explicitly by the
adverbial *ʾûlay*; it refers to a future possibility. The quotation may then constitute a purpose sequence: "Perhaps he can be fooled so that we can prevail
over him, and take our revenge on him" (I owe this grammatical point to
Monsignor P. K. Skehan). Kelly (1920:15) takes this case as "causal" and
would translate "therefore" before the second verb. On the textual witness
to "Yahweh of hosts" in v 12, see Janzen 1973:79. The translation of v 11
renders *ʿôlām* adverbially. The second occurrence of *yhwh* in v 13 (cf. *ʾtw* reflected in LXX; cf. Janzen 1973:74) is sometimes deleted by scholars, but is
retained here.

Like the first and fourth laments, the final lament opens, using the
active and passive forms of the same verb. In the first lines in these laments, the invocation of Yahweh stands between the two occurrences of
the same verb. The first section of the final lament, verses 7-10, recapitu-
lates the history of Jeremiah's prophetic life. Yahweh made him be a
prophet (v 7a; cf. Clines and Gunn 1978:20-24); for this reason he is
ridiculed all the time (v 7b). When he speaks the word of destruction for
Judah (v 8a), it shows how Yahweh's word has turned him into a social
outcast (v 8b). And when Jeremiah thinks not to speak out anymore in
the name of Yahweh (v 9a), he cannot help himself; he must speak (v 9b;
cf. Amos 3:8). V 10 depicts the enemies, now including his friends, talk-
ing about his demise. This section is centered on verbal discourse. It is
crowded with words of speaking: "to mock" (**lʿg*) in v 7; "to speak"

(*dbr) in vv 8 and 9 and "word" (děbar) of Yahweh in v 8; "to cry out" (*z῾q) and "to shout" (*qrʾ) in v 8; "to say" (*ʾmr) and "to mention" (*zkr) in v 9; "to denounce" (*ngd) in v 10. Vv 7-10 illustrates how discourse is leading to the prophet's demise: Jeremiah's speaking for Yahweh causes enemies' speaking about Jeremiah.

What is at stake is a matter of discourse, and this discourse becomes a matter of life and death for the enemies in vv 11-12. The second section of the final lament in vv 11-12 changes the direction of the discourse, opening with a note of Yahweh as help. Here Yahweh is compared to the "strong warrior" (gibbôr ῾ārîṣ), a role frequently attributed to Yahweh in poetic material. Exod 15:3, for example, calls Yahweh "a man of war" (ʾîš milḥāmâ). Because Jeremiah is precisely Yahweh's prophet, the prophet has a basis for his prayer of deliverance. There is a wordplay which reinforces precisely this relationship between the prophetic mission and Yahweh's ability as warrior to save the prophet. In v 9, the fire which is the need to prophesy is "shut up" (῾āṣūr) in Jeremiah's bones; in v 11 Yahweh is called to be a "strong" (῾ārîṣ) warrior. The phonetic resemblance between these two words draws attention to their intimate thematic resonance: Jeremiah calls on Yahweh to be ῾ārîṣ for him because Yahweh made him ῾āṣūr. And this call implies the destruction of his enemies who threaten the prophet's life. In v 12 Jeremiah cries out to Yahweh to "take vengeance" (*nqm) upon his enemies, just as they intended to "take vengeance" (*nqm) against him in v 10 (Pitard 1982:23). These two uses of *nqm clearly pose an adversarial relationship between the prophet and the people.

Two verbal roots, *pth, "to fool," and *ykl, "to be able," also constitute important indicators of meaning in this lament (Clines and Gunn 1976:396). In punctuating this lament, the two verbs chart the course of the poem in form as well as content. V 7 speaks of how Yahweh "fooled" (*pth) and "prevailed over" (*ykl) him. V 9 repeats the root *ykl, "to be able," and adds poetic punch to the message by playing on this verb with a similar sounding verb, kalkēl, "to contain" (*kwl). Jeremiah speaks of the physical necessity of fulfilling his prophetic role of speaking to the people. He says first: "I was weary holding it in (nilʾêtî kalkēl). Then he says loʾ ʾûkāl, either "I was helpless" (NJPS); or "I cannot" hold it in any longer (RSV).

Levenson (1984) has noted a deeper paranomasia involving the words ʾûkāl and kalkēl in v 9. The words can be taken in the sense indicated by the MT pointing: Jeremiah is weary with containing the word. Or, the two words can also be read with two most minimal interpretive moves, altering the vocalization of *ʾûkāl* to *ʾukkal*, and taking *kalkēl* in its second meaning, "to feed." Hence the sentence would also mean: "I am tired of feeding when I do not eat." With this wordplay, the sense is that Jeremiah cannot contain the word, nor can it sustain him. Levenson (1984:225) sees in the conjunction of fire and the divine word in 20:9 an allusion to the commission of Moses: in contrast to Moses, "Jeremiah who has eaten the word (Jer 15:16) and tried to proclaim it (20:8), finds himself 'exhausted' (*nilʾêtî*, v. 9)." From this perspective, Jeremiah is a type, or more precisely an anti-type, to Moses (cf. Holladay 1964,1966; Seitz 1989a). It is clear that the prophet stands at the mercy of Yahweh. In v 10 the enemies threaten by planning to "fool" (**pth*) and "prevail" (**ykl*) over the prophet. Finally, in v 11 the prophet prays that the enemies "will be incapable" (*loʾ yūkālû*) of hurting him in the end.

The repetition of **pth*, "to fool," and **ykl*, "to be able," provides a structural and thematic thread for the poem. First, in v 7 it sets the tone for the whole of the lament. Jeremiah stands in his present situation because Yahweh made it happen this way; Yahweh fooled and overpowered him. The poem as a whole develops this theme. Second, the verbs in v 9 reinforce the fact that Yahweh's superior power made Jeremiah continue as a prophet: there was nothing that he could do to escape this fate. Jeremiah served as a prophet only because of Yahweh; otherwise, he would not be in this predicament. Third, the repetition of the two verbs yet again in v 10 implicitly compares the treatment which the prophet receives from Yahweh in v 7 to the treatment which he knows his enemies plan for him in v 10. Finally, it should be noted that the particle *kōl*, "all, every" related to *kalkēl* and similar in sound to **ykl*, punctuates this poem (O'Connor 1988:68). The prophet is mocked "all" day, and "everyone" mocks him (v 7). The word of Yahweh has become a source of scorn "all" day (v 8). It is "all" of the prophet's friends who denounce him (v 10). The number of other words or word-groups with the consonants /k/ and /l/ is unusual (see Diamond 1987:252 n. 12). V 11 has an especially conspicuous series of repetitions of these two consonants: *ʿal-kēn*, "therefore"; twice in *kî-lōʾ hiśkîlû* and then again *kĕlimmat*, "humiliation" (note also /l/ and /k/ in the cluster, *ʿôlām lōʾ tiśśākēaḥ*, "will never be forgotten"). V 12 invokes the righteous judge who sees the heart but also the *kĕlāyôt*, literally "kidneys," a synonym for the personal dimension of Jeremiah. The two verbal roots and other similarly sounding words tie the complaint in vv 7-10 with the final prophetic call for vengeance in vv 11-12.

V 13 stands at the point where a divine response might appear, compared with most of the earlier laments. Instead, there is a call to prayer, a feature found in some individual laments (O'Connor 1988:69, 70-71, 94). The verse presupposes a positive divine response. According to O'Connor (1988:69), the verse may serve to mark the prophet's final deliverance from his enemies.

The internal content of the laments sometimes involves a defense of Jeremiah's prophetic ministry. The issue which causes persecution of Jeremiah is precisely his prophetic mission (15:16; 17:16; 18:20; 20:8-9; cf. 11:21). According to the concrete circumstances known of the prophet's life, his enemies involved those members of the Jerusalemite establishment who opposed his prophetic mission; this could have included some of his own relations (Wilson 1980:230-35, 241-51). Diamond (1987:33-35, 50-51, 77-78, 81, 100, 113-14, 127-91, 212 n. 46) also stresses both the proximate threats of the prophet's kinsmen in the first lament and the more general threat of the people as a whole. O'Connor (1988:26, 42, 50, 58, 71-72, 85-96, 97, 103) further emphasizes the threats of false prophets based on the oracle against false prophecy in Jer 23:18-22. O'Connor's exegesis of the laments' function partially depends on viewing them in terms of prophetic conflict, a theme never mentioned as such in the laments. Although the unnamed enemies could have included "false" prophets, Jeremiah himself stresses those who oppose his oracles of judgement. Jer 18:20 identifies the enemies as those on whose behalf he interceded before Yahweh; these are hardly other prophets. Apart from the reference to the "men of Anathoth" in the first lament, Diamond recognizes the rather general characterizations of the enemies within the laments. In his review of Diamond's 1987 study of Jeremiah, Stulman (1989:317-18) claims that different laments serve different functions:

> ...the confessions, in my opinion, are far too diverse and complex to be subsumed under a single rubric or literary function...Several poems, for example, depict Jeremiah as the paradigm of the suffering servant...; others serve as a defense for Jeremiah's prophetic integrity...; still others are apparently intended to shatter popular notions regarding the Zion-temple cult. All of these motifs seems [sic] to *stand on their own without any direct dependence upon the theodicy theme.* (Stulman's italics)

There is little or no basis for arguing that some laments are aimed at ideas about Zion or the temple cult (although poems other than the laments in chapters 11-20 address this theme, e.g. 11:15-16). The notion that Jeremiah is described as a "suffering servant" may be challenged in view of the differences between the two figures (noted above); if it were an appropriate comparison, this interpretation of Jeremiah would fit with the defense of his prophetic mission.

Jeremiah claims to be hounded by enemies largely left unnamed, but mentioned in all of the laments. His identity as a prophet is threatened since his message of judgement, questioned by these enemies, has not come to pass (17:16). Is Jeremiah's prophecy true or not? If so, why has it not come to pass? If not, how can he be called a true prophet of Yahweh? The laments attempt to mediate this difficulty by exploring the problems which Jeremiah faced as a prophet. The answer lies in how his prophetic ministry defies some of the norms customary for a prophet, such as intercession and identification with the people. While more recent scholars have demurred from the older view of the laments as genuine psychological portraits of the prophet (e.g., Skinner 1922; see Diamond 1987:11-16), the portraits function to persuade the audience of Jeremiah's authenticity as a prophet, and the psychological dimension expressed in the laments aids the strategy of persuasion (Diamond 1987:120). The divine responses to the laments also address the issue of the prophet's apparent failure. As Holladay (1986:360-61) has observed, the few divine answers to Jeremiah's laments stand in tension with one another: they proclaim assurance and announce persecution for the prophet.

The present order of the laments and the ending of 20:13 may function as a defense of the prophetic ministry (O'Connor 1988:69, 157), but such a view is problematic on a number of grounds. The first difficulty lies in the content. In general, if 20:13 functions as the conclusion to the lament material, then the prophet is defended with a positive ending, but this interpretation in part assumes that the present order of the laments is original (so O'Connor 1988:157; cf. Diamond 1987:130-46; 1989:696). The lack of an antecedent for the pronominal suffix in "their deeds" (11:18) would suggest the secondary nature of the present context of 11:18-23 (McKane 1986:254-55), and there are no indications internal to the laments that the original order was preserved (Diamond 1987:145; Overholt 1988:619). Some scholars also view the "progression" of the laments in very different terms than O'Connor. If 20:14-18 is to be included with the laments, as O'Connor argues, the picture is one of an increasingly more threatening situation (Overholt 1988:619).

Furthermore, it is evident that the laments have been situated with other material from the Jeremianic tradition. Indeed, the precise relationship of the laments themselves to the prophet cannot be easily ascertained. While O'Connor attributes the laments and their present order to the prophet himself, Diamond is more reserved on this point. Although the laments belong to Jeremianic tradition, there is no guarantee that the prophet authored all of the laments. Indeed, for Carroll and Pohlmann, the laments are secondary compositions. While it is possible to identify secondary features within the laments, it appears impossible either to pinpoint the settings for these additions or to adjudicate the questions of authorship; the present context of the book is not focused on recovering the *ipsissima verba* of the prophet. Indeed, the laments belong to contexts which offer different clues about their interpretation.

TWO

⟣⟨⟨⟩⟩⟢

The Units within Jeremiah 11-20

1. CRITERIA FOR DETERMINING UNITS

The context of Jeremiah's laments plays a major role in determining their sense and function within the book of Jeremiah. The immediate context of the laments, chapters 11-20, contains highly diverse material, and understanding these chapters involves the issue of delineating the units within them. This is an especially crucial issue for interpreting the laments, especially as current scholarship shows little unanimity over this issue. Recent interpretations (Diamond 1987; O'Connor 1988) of the laments in their contexts are premised on the division of chapters 11-20, yet the two studies differ markedly over the boundaries of the larger units within these chapters. If the units which provide the context for the laments are controverted, then the meaning of the context remains in part a moot issue. Determining the units within Jeremiah 11-20 is therefore necessary before addressing other aspects of the laments' context. The issues involved are complex; the task is to make sense out of the "untidy accumulation of material," again to mention McKane's description of the entire book (McKane 1981:228; see Carroll 1986:43).

There have been four major approaches to the question of the larger units within Jeremiah 11-20. First, some scholars prescind from the issue. In his commentary, McKane, for example, does not offer divisions of the units. Second, some scholars offer thematic criteria for delineating units. Holladay (1976:145-63) presents a complex thematic approach to chapters 11-20. He isolates six thematic complexes belonging to an initial stratum (for discussion, see Diamond 1987:133-34). Following a long line of interpretation, O'Connor (1988:135-38; cf. McKane 1986:lxvi) sees chapter 16 as a development of, or what she calls a "midrash" on, the theme of chapter 15 (see McKane 1986:366). The topic of the social life of the people provides some measure of continuity between chapters 15 and 16. Third, commentators offer structural criteria for dividing chapters 11-20. For example, on the basis of superscriptions in 11:1, 14:1 and 18:1, Carroll (1986; 1989:44-46) and Diamond divide the chapters into 11-13, 14-17 and 18-20 with two laments in each of these three units. O'Connor splits the material differently: 11-12, 13, 14-16, 17, 18-20. Like Carroll and Diamond, O'Connor views 11:1, 14:1 and 18:1 as the beginnings of units on the basis of the superscriptions in these verses. Fourth, there have been attempts to see a larger structural pattern common to the major sections in chapters 11-20. According to Thiel (1973:287), the following elements are common to the units consisting of chapters 11-12, 14-15, 18 and 19-20: occasion for preaching; message of judgement; word of judgement; persecution of prophet; and lament.

All of these approaches have their merits. The first approach may represent the better part of wisdom. There are numerous difficulties involved in delimiting the units within chapters 11-20. The material in Jeremiah 11-20 derives from a variety of historical periods. The literary relationships within the chapters are complex, and any attempt to render a literary order or historical reconstruction is fraught with potential difficulties. The first approach thus counsels caution in proceeding with this issue. The second approach likewise has its advantages. It provides some explanation for grouping of material despite the diversity of passages. The third approach is also important. Superscriptions and other structural features provide some markers designating the units inherent in chapters 11-20. The fourth approach represents an attempt to provide a comprehensive solution, embracing all the material in the chapters. The advantages of these approaches are to be included in any attempt to delineate the units within chapters 11-20.

The difficulties with these interpretive strategies are likewise apparent. The first approach does not address the problem and therefore it offers no hope of a solution. Either the chapters are left to be read as a synchronic whole — a difficult proposition at best (cf. Heschel 1962:103-39); or they remain a group of undefined or unrelated units whose reasons for arrangement — and therefore in part their meaning — remain unknown (cf. Overholt 1988:616-28). The use of thematic criteria in the second approach also runs into some problems. From O'Connor's division, chapters 14-16 constitutes a unit, which leaves 13 and 17 as isolated pieces. The problem for chapter 17 is especially conspicuous, as it has no superscription. The lack of a superscription may indicate that chapter 17 is not a separate unit, returning the discussion to the conclusion that chapters 14-17 function as a unit, precisely the view of McKane and Diamond. One problem with Diamond's view is that his grouping of such large units makes it difficult to discern structure within these units (von Waldow 1989:126), apart from his argument that two laments are deliberately placed in each major unit. What of the rest of the material within each unit and its relationship to the laments? The unwieldy character of the material within such large units proposed by Diamond perhaps partakes of McKane's position that the material is too uneven literarily and historically to permit an ordering. The third approach to the material through the superscriptions is a partial one at best, and represents only a starting point. The various purposes and dates of the many superscriptions are unclear. Seitz (1989b:230 n. 49) so comments on the superscriptions in 11:1, 18:1, 21:1 and elsewhere: "These introductory forms are too general, however, to develop a rigid redactional theory." The superscriptions may serve as a guide to dividing material in chapters 11-20, therefore, only in conjunction with other evidence. The fourth approach represented by Thiel's work has been criticized on a number of grounds. Diamond (1987:151-52, 160) and O'Connor (1988:116-17) largely attack Thiel's problematic assignments of material based on his own form-critical categories. There is the further difficulty of the place of chapters 13 and 17, a problem looming also in O'Connor's analysis.

Any attempt to render order from the apparent chaos of the material in Jeremiah 11-20 is fraught with major obstacles. Indeed, the literary and historical issues are complex; they complicate any proposed solution. As this discussion of the units demonstrates, delineating units is a difficult enterprise. The process of dividing chapters 11-20 into units may unknowingly and falsely harmonize a variety of literary stages or deny others as well, or perhaps even reconstruct yet others which may never have existed. In short, tracing the growth of Jeremiah 11-20 is an impossible task due to the multiple levels of tradition which are too obscure to identify. It may be possible, however, to set the delineation of the major units within Jeremiah 11-20 on a firmer footing, which would represent a first step in trying to understand the complex nature of these chapters.

2. THE UNITS: CHAPTERS 11-12, 13-15, 16-17, AND 18-20

Superscriptions have long served as the basic criterion for division of chapters 11-20. They continue to represent a starting point for dividing the chapters, if only because they mark explicitly the beginning of units. MT Jeremiah 11-20 contains a number of superscriptions which may function on various levels (for retroversions based on LXX, see Varughese. 1984:91, 103, 115, 126, 140, 144, 154, 170-73; Running 1985:228):

11:1   MT: "The word that was to Jeremiah from Yahweh, saying..."

haddābār ʾăšer hāyâ ʾel-yirmĕyāhû mēʾēt yhwh lēʾmor

LXX: "The word that was from Yahweh to Jeremiah, saying..."

haddābār ʾăšer hāyâ mēʾēt yhwh ʾel-yirmĕyāhû lēʾmōr

13:1   MT: "Thus said Yahweh to me..."

kōh-ʾāmar yhwh ʾēlay

4QJer^a: kh ʾmr yhwh ʾ[ ]

(LXX has nothing corresponding to MT ʾēlay)

14:1   MT: "...which was the word of Yahweh to Jeremiah concerning the matters of the droughts..."

ʾăšer hāyâ dĕbar-yhwh ʾel-yirmĕyāhû
ʿal-dibrê habbaṣṣārôt

LXX: "And the word of Yahweh was to Jeremiah concerning the droughts..."

wayhî dĕbar-yhwh ʾel-yirmĕyāhû ʿal habbaṣṣārôt

15:1   MT & LXX: "And Yahweh said to me..."

wayyōʾmer yhwh ʾēlay

16:1   MT: "And the word of Yahweh was to me, saying..."

wayhî dĕbar-yhwh ʾēlay lēʾmōr

LXX: no superscription

17:19   MT: "Thus Yahweh said to me..."

kōh-ʾāmar yhwh ʾēlay

4QJer^a: kh ʾmr yhwh [ ]y

LXX zero for MT *ʾēlay*

18:1   MT: "The word that was to Jeremiah from Yahweh, saying..."
              haddābār ʾăšer hāyâ ʾel-yirmĕyāhû mēʾēt yhwh lēʾmōr
       LXX: "The word that was from Yahweh to Jeremiah, saying..."
              haddābār ʾăšer hāyâ mēʾēt yhwh ʾel-yirmĕyāhû lēʾmōr

19:1   MT: "Thus Yahweh said..."
              kōh ʾāmar yhwh
       LXX: "Then Yahweh said to me..."
              ʾaz ʾāmar yhwh ʾēlay

21:1   MT: "The word that was to Jeremiah from Yahweh...saying..."
              haddābār ʾăšer hāyâ ʾel-yirmĕyāhû mēʾēt yhwh...lēʾmōr
       LXX: "The word that was from Yahweh to Jeremiah, saying..."
              haddābār ʾăšer hāyâ mēʾēt yhwh ʾel-yirmĕyāhû lēʾmōr

The superscriptions in 11:1,18:1 and 21:1 demarcate new units. The other superscriptions are less clear. The ones in 13:1 and 15:1 differ from 11:1, 18:1 and 21:1; neither of the two mention the prophet. This difference might imply another level of division. Yet assuming that 13:1 and 15:1 begin sections (as O'Connor argues for 13:1) is problematic. If 13:1 reflects a new unit, what is the significance of the difference in this superscription compared to those in 11:1, 18:1 and 21:1? Does the superscription of 13:1 represent a different editorial level or function? The superscription in 13:1 is identical to that of 17:19, which appears to be a postexilic addition (Carroll 1986:368; Holladay 1986:509; McKane 1986:417-18; Overholt 1988: 623; see Introduction). Jer 15:1 is more problematic than 13:1. In its present position, this superscription links the prayer of the people in 14:19-22 to Yahweh's rejection of the people's prayer in 15:1. McKane (1986:lxvi) argues for a more integral relationship between 15:1 and the preceding unit; he proposes that 14:17-21 generated 15:1-4. While the superscriptions of 11:1, 18:1 and 21:1 evidently constitute the most basic markers of unit divisions, the superscriptions of chapters 13-17 and their editorial function(s) remain somewhat problematic. The differences in the superscriptions suggest that either 14:1 has a different editorial function from 11:1 or 18:1 (and hence the division at 14:1 should be abandoned), or the superscriptions of 11:1, 18:1 and 21:1 represent a different editorial level or stage from 14:1; or both factors are possibilities.

Perhaps the "general untidyness" of the material, at least insofar as it involves the superscriptions, should be conceded.

From this reading of the superscriptions thus far, it might be inferred
that the units are 11-12, 13-15, 16-17 and 18-20. The division of chapters
11-20 into these four units would have two apparent problems, however.
A great number of commentators claim that the superscription in 14:1
delineates a new unit (Diamond 1987:149; cf. O'Connor 1988:135).
Moreover, O'Connor has noted the continuity of themes between chapters 15 and 16. These links include the motif of destruction in 15:3 and
16:4 and the image of mother in 15:8-10 and 16:3 (Carroll 1986:338). Yet
these two problems may be mirages. The superscription in 14:1 varies
formally from all of the other superscriptions. It begins with the problematic ʾăšer hāyâ, "which was," the sort of relative clause which would
otherwise have an antecedent (cf. *wayhî underlying LXX and Syriac; see
Varughese 1984:171). In commenting on Jer 46:1, Janzen (1973:113-14)
notes: "The secondary character of the sentence is further suggested by
the fact that not one of the אשר היה דבר־יהוה formulas (14.1, 46.1, 47.1, 49.34)
is textually stable." Janzen thus argues that 14:1 represents a secondary
expansion. Whichever textual version is superior (assuming there is one),
the superscription differs from all the others in chapters 11-20 and would
appear to be secondary. Furthermore, the superscription in 14:1 states
explicitly that it concerns the drought, described only in chapter 14.
Hence 14:1 is not a superscription for a unit longer than this chapter. In
short, chapter 14 does not begin a larger unit despite the opinions of a
number of scholars to the contrary (e.g., Rudolph 1968:110; del Olmo
Lete 1971; Diamond 1987; O'Connor 1988). Indeed, Diamond (1987:150)
observes that 13:1f. "appears to offer a break" and that connections between 14:1f. and the preceding chapters are lacking.

A further question surrounds positing 16:1 as the beginning of a new
unit. As O'Connor argues, major thematic links bind chapters 15 and 16.
These links could be viewed as connections between sections and rather
than parts belonging to the same unit. Or, a diachronic explanation could
obviate the difficulty of suggesting that 16:1 constitutes a new unit.
Chapter 16 could have been generated as an elaboration on 15:17, a stage
which Holladay (1986:358) views as early. Chapter 16 later received the
superscription which demarcates it as a new unit. The continuity of
theme between chapters 15 and 16 need not pose a significant
impediment to the position that 16:1 begins a new unit. By the same
reasoning which O'Connor offers against assigning 16:1 as the beginning
of a new unit, chapter 17 could not begin a new unit, as O'Connor ar-

gues, because of the links between 16:19 and 17:17 (although these links are not as strong as those drawn by O'Connor between the end of chapter 15 and the beginning of chapter 16). Other motifs span a number of units (e.g., the image of Yahweh as water in 15:18 and 17:8, 13; the ubiquitous theme of knowledge in 11:18, 16:21, etc.; the theme of the tree and its fruit in 11:19, 12:2 and 17:8).

There is another issue in positing 16:1 as the beginning of a new unit. The superscription in Jer 16:1 does not appear in LXX of Jeremiah (Janzen 1973:113; Tov 1981:152; Stulman 1985:67; Varughese 1984:174). The textual witnesses to this verse would presuppose that either the MT attestation to the superscription postdates the production of the LXX or it belonged to a separate, early MT tradition. The former option seems more likely (Tov 1981:150-67; 1985:218). The post-exilic addition of MT 16:1 appears to be an attempt to provide order to the highly varied Jeremianic traditions attested in chapters 11-20, a move congruent with other additions to MT not found in LXX.

Given the late date of MT 16:1, the present arrangement of superscriptions in MT involved at least a late phase; indeed, 13:1 and 17:19, identical in form, seem to stem from the post-exilic period (see Tov 1981:166). The superscriptions represent one of the later elements joined to the material to give it order, and 13:1, 16:1 and 17:19 are distinctly different in character from 11:1, 18:1 and 21:1, which might be considered earlier. In general, the superscriptions serve as explicit markers of context and order, secondarily imposed upon a vast array of diverse traditional material. To the degree that this is true, the arrangement of material in MT Jeremiah 11-20 is late. Hence, examining the context of the laments involves looking back in time from the latest stages of additional material, including the superscriptions, refracted though many levels of tradition (although the background of these levels is not revealed in the text; cf. Tov 1985:216, figure 1). The superscriptions themselves illustrate this degree of complexity. MT 16:1 constitutes a late divider perhaps added to render order within chapters 13-17. While 11:1, 18:1 and 21:1 represent older markers, 13:1 and 16:1 were inserted (at different stages?) to provide clarity for the material intervening (or further added to?) between the units earlier intended to be marked by 11:1 and 18:1. Indeed, earlier units within chapters 13-17 (such as 14:1-15:3 or 14:1-15:9 as proposed by a number of scholars; see the commentaries) may have become so laden with additional material that new markers of units became useful. The various questions involving the different superscriptions perhaps indicate the limited value which they provide for reconstructing

the units of the book's "first edition" (see Tov 1981, 1985). The superscriptions made explicit the divisions of the major sections that may have
been implicit at an earlier stage. In other words, the addition of the superscription in 16:1 by the "second edition" perhaps represented an interpretation of the "first" edition's grouping of the material in chapters
11-20.

The complications surrounding the various dates and forms of the
superscriptions indicate the limitations which they have as indicators of
structure. As a result, other factors require consideration. Thiel (1973:287)
based his division of the material on a larger arrangement and not on superscriptions alone. While his attempt was criticized (see Diamond
1987:151-52; O'Connor 1988:116-17), his approach may point in the right
direction. At the same time, various editorial levels have to be kept in
mind while making such arrangements of material and in drawing any
conclusions from these arrangements. Bearing in mind these textual
complexities and historical unknowns, dividing chapters 11-20 into four
units, chapters 11-12, 13-15, 16-17, and 18-20, may serve as a working
hypothesis. The basis for this division does not depend primarily on the
superscriptions; rather, there are other reasons for proposing these four
units. Indeed, there are a number of structural points in common among
these four units. First, each section commences with a superscription
(11:1; 13:1; 16:1; 18:1). Second, each superscription of each section is
followed by a prose section. These sections largely condemn Israel in
Deuteronomistic language (Robert 1943; Rudolph 1968:77, 91, 109-110;
Thiel 1973:139-57, 169-76, 195-201, 210-18; Weinfeld 1976:221). In 13:1f.,
16:1f., and 18:1f., each prose section illustrates the condemnation by
means of a "symbol" (for the complexities of the material in these prose
sections, see the commentaries). In chapter 13, this is the waistcloth, in
chapter 16 the command not to take a wife, and in chapter 18:1 the image
of the potter (this theme is amplified in 19:1f.). The initial unit, 11:1f. departs from this plan. Third, each of the four units begins with two commands (expressed either as an imperative plus converted imperfect, as in
11:2, 13:1 and 18:2, or in the case of 16:2, two volitives, $lō^{\circ}$ $tiqqaḥ$, "you
shall not take..." and $lō^{\circ}$-$yihyû$ $lĕkā$, "you shall not have..."). These commands appear in large measure as a function of their immediate settings
at the beginning of the stories. Nonetheless, they add to the impression
of balance among the four units.

If the prose sections at the beginning of the units have been specially
positioned with a particular function in relation to the laments
(O'Connor 1988:112), then other similar prose sections in 17:19-27 and

19:1f. require explanation. These two sections are built secondarily on other pieces within the larger units to which they belong. Jer 17:19-27, which reports Israel's violation of the Shabbat, is designed perhaps to provide a basis for the indictment of Israel in 16:11 (Weinfeld 1976:55; Carroll 1986:368; Holladay 1986:509; McKane 1986:417-18; cf. Overholt 1988:623; see the Introduction). Jer 19:1f. is a second potter story parallel to 18:1f. (Thiel 1973:161-62, 228-29; Diamond 1987:172). Bracketing these two sections for a moment, a fourth structural element appears in the arrangement of the four units, and this is the placement of the prophetic laments. The four major sections apparently end with a prophetic lament if the units at the end of the first, third and fourth sections (12:7-17; 17:19-27; 20:14-18) are secondary (see chapter three). This view is inherent in Thiel's delineation of units (1973:287) noted above, and O'Connor (1988:113) has observed the relationship between the introductory units and the prophetic laments. Similarly, Childs (1979:347-48) has remarked on the Deuteronomistic interpretation of the prophet provided by the placement of these prose narratives in conjunction with the laments. It is possible that this juxtaposition of introductory stories and laments in the four units represents a redactional stage, but there is no means to verify such a stage in the redactional history of chapters 11-20.

The placement of the initial announcement of judgement stresses the theme of judgement and provides a new departure for the understanding of the laments (Diamond 1987:183). The laments now placed with the introductory prose sections illustrate how the condition of the prophet reflects divine judgement against the people. Thanks to the juxtaposition of the introductory narratives with the laments, the introductory stories accent the guilt of Jeremiah's enemies, presumed to be the same adversaries denounced in the laments. As a result, there is a shift from the laments' original purpose to their main function in context. In their original usage, they serve to defend Jeremiah's prophetic mission against unnamed enemies. In context, however, the laments stress the guilt of the prophet's foes and extend their identity to include Judah and Jerusalem, in short all the people and its leadership (11:2; 13:13; 18:6, 11; 19:3). In sum, the laments in context announce that the persecution of Yahweh's prophet deserves the punishment of Yahweh's people.

3. THE FUNCTION OF INTRODUCTORY STORY
PLUS PROPHETIC LAMENT

The units of Jeremiah 11-12, 13-15, 16-17 and 18-20 share a basic structure of organization. Each of these four sections has two parts: an introductory prose narrative plus prophetic lament (cf. O'Connor 1988:130-31). The identification of this organization within the four sections of Jeremiah 11-20 is important for a number of reasons. It serves to identify the pattern of the material of chapters 11-20. Furthermore, it may clarify some principles behind the arrangement of these chapters.

This basic pattern of which the laments are a part suggest a further function apart from their original use. Rather than defend Jeremiah's prophetic ministry, the laments function in context to accent the guilt of the people, pointing to the necessity of the exile (O'Connor 1988:158). The linkage between the introductory story and the laments is provided by the references to the enemies in the laments. The enemies of the laments are implicitly understood at this stage of the tradition to refer to those mentioned in the introductory prophetic stories. No lament names the enemies. In the first lament, only the divine answer, which looks like a secondary prose piece specially tailored to its context, identifies the enemies. These are the people of Jeremiah's hometown (Jer 11:21, 23). Otherwise, in the laments the enemies remain unnamed evildoers. The impression of the prose section following the fourth lament is that Jeremiah faces the inhabitants of Jerusalem and the southern kingdom of Judah. Later prose sections depict the sufferings which Jeremiah endures from people of his hometown and from political circles of Judah so that the divine answers to the laments correlate with the prose chronicles of Jeremiah's life contained in later chapters of the book. Yet the enemies within the poetic body of the laments remain unnamed. The enemies in both the prose divine answers and poetic laments are important. The identified enemies are important for their historical value. They give a specific account of the life of Jeremiah and the rejection of his prophetic ministry. They name the guilty parties, both within the prophet's whole family, and within the national political leadership. They "name names." This specificity assigns responsibility for the rejection of Jeremiah and thereby Yahweh, and therefore explains the national calamity of the exile. This leads to the further importance of the unnamed enemies. It may be that the non-referential quality of the enemies within the body of the laments would have seemed to apply to the enemies named in the prose divine answers; otherwise the divine prose answers would fit less well with the laments.

The context of the final lament in Jer 20:7-13, beginning in 20:1-6, plays an important role in the treatment of the enemies. Before chapter 20 no enemies were explicitly named. The closest explicit mention of enemies were "the men of Anathoth" in the divine answer to the first lament (Jer 11:21-23), itself an addition to make concrete the identity of the enemies named in the laments (Diamond 1987:23-28; McKane 1986:255; O'Connor 1988:18). In chapter 20, the context of the final lament begins to specify the enemies. Prior to chapter 20, the other laments present the righteousness of Jeremiah before Yahweh over and against unnamed enemies, and these speeches strike at the need to destroy the enemies; indeed, they hint at the inevitability of destruction. The context for the last lament opens a new chapter even as it closes an old one. As it completes the cycle of individual prophetic laments, it begins a new part of the book of Jeremiah that lays out in great detail the burden and responsibility for Judah's exile, first in 597 and then in 587/586, issuing in the destruction of Jerusalem. Chapter 20 begins to name names and make clear who bears the responsibility for Judah's fall. One function of the cycle of laments is to prepare the audience for the identity of the enemies. Up to this point, the identity of the guilty has been largely left unrevealed all the while their guilt has been made indelible.

The "enemies" presented in the laments opposed the true word of Yahweh embodied in the prophet's message; moreover, their refusal to hear his word resulted in their following false prophets. The enemies largely left unnamed in the laments emerge in the following narratives as the nation's leaders — all the people (cf. 11:2; 13:13; 18:6, 11; 19:3), including priests, prophets and kings (Seitz 1989b:11, 20, 86). In context the laments of Jeremiah partake of a larger purpose of illustrating the necessity of national exile. By themselves the laments validate Jeremiah as Yahweh's true prophet within his own lifetime. With emphasis placed in the prose sections on the enemies and the failure of the nation to heed the words of the prophet, the laments take on additional meaning for understanding the fall of the southern kingdom. In short, one function of the laments in their immediate context is to "illustrate...the indictment of Israel and explain the disaster which finally overtook the nation" (O'Connor 1988:113; cf. 158; Diamond 1987:56). As announcements of judgement, the divine speeches in the prose stories provide an interpretive setting for the laments. These speeches invoke the people's breaking of the covenant (11:3, 8). The people's main sin is seeking after other deities (11:12-13, 17; 13:10; 16:11), to a degree even worse than their fathers (16:12; cf. 11:7). These announcements of judgement also paint pictures of Israel's destruction (11:16; 13:12-14; 16:4, 9, 16f.).

The laments are connected to these themes in the introductory sections not only structurally, but also through some thematic and verbal links between them. In the first section, the redactional comment of 11:21-23 connects the laments to the theme of Israel's failure to hear in 11:1-14 (O'Connor 1988:105). Moreover, the judgement on the house (*bêt*) of Israel and Judah in 11:10 reverberates in 12:6, 7 (O'Connor 1988:106). In the second main section, chapters 13-15, the theme of evil links the introductory section with the prophetic lament. In section three, chapters 16-17, the day of judgement in 17:16 represents a national calamity explicitly described in 16:4. Finally, the two structures of chapters 18-20 connect the initial potter stories with the laments. Jer 18:1-11 and 18:19-23 voice themes of evil and destruction. 19:1-13 illustrates some of the "violence" which the prophet denounces in 20:8. Hence, national sin becomes the referent for the prophetic criticism. On the whole, national sin and destruction become the dominant referent of the prophetic laments. The laments, viewed through the themes in the introductory stories, become vehicles of national judgement.

THREE

❖

The Divine Speeches in Chapters 11-20

The previous chapter isolated one pattern of material within Jeremiah 11-20, which may be schematized in the following manner:

Section I: Chapters 11-12
    1. 11:1-12: Announcement of judgement
    2. 11:18-23: Prophetic lament
Section II: Chapters 13-15
    1. 13:1-11: Action illustrating judgement
    2. 15:15-21: Prophetic lament
Section III: Chapters 16-17
    1. 16:1-9: Actions illustrating announcement
    2. 17:14-18: Prophetic lament
Section IV: Chapters 18-20
    1. 18:1-12: Action illustrating announcement
    2. 20:7-13: Prophetic lament

The fit of introductory announcement plus prophetic lament was complicated by the insertion of two additional laments. According to Bright (1965:84-90), Rudolph (1968:75-76) and Janzen (1973:132), there are signs of textual dislocation within 12:1-6 (see also Overholt 1988:617). Bright considers v 4 to be Jeremiah's words drawn from another context. The placement of two laments together in this case is unique to the corpus and was due likely to secondary placement. Chapters 18-20 contain the introductory prose piece plus prophetic lament twice, thus including an additional lament. The two curses of Jer 15:10-14 and 20:14-18 also complicate the arrangement of the units to which they belong, and provide further determination of the meaning of the units.

Against the background of this patterning of material, it is possible to clarify the arrangement of other material contained in chapters 11-20. This formulation need not imply that this pattern had a redactional priority, i.e., that this pattern was an intermediate redactional stage in the development of chapters 11-20. There is no way to verify such a suggestion; and there is no way of knowing what other units of material within chapters 11-20 were attached to one another, prior to the arrangement of introductory prose piece plus prophetic lament. The bulk of the further additions are the divine speeches and the speeches of either the people or the prophet. The types of connections between these speeches and the laments have been summarized by O'Connor (1988:111-12). First, three of the laments (11:18-12:6; 15:10-21; 20:7-13) are tied to their immediate context through catchwords. Second, 11:18-12:6 and 15:10-21 share images and motifs with their surrounding contexts. Third, 11:18-12:6 and 18:18-23 are meshed further with their contexts by means of redactional comments added to them. The connections noted in the following sections include verbal and thematic associations between not only the laments and their most immediate contexts, but also among the various units in the context and the impact which these connections have on the interpretation of the laments in context. Many of these connections have been noted by commentators (e.g., Diamond 1987:149-75; O'Connor 1988:104-13). A section-by-section review of the divine speeches and the accompanying material illustrates some of the structural arrangements and the connections between all of the various units in chapters 11-20, including the laments.

1. CHAPTERS 11-12

The initial prose piece of 11:1-14 is a complex piece consisting of several smaller units (see McKane 1986:lxxi-lxxii). Vv 1-5 report an oracle which is to be announced. The unit has a double introduction (vv 1, 3). The message that follows in vv 3b-5 proclaims the people's violation of the covenant which Yahweh made with the patriarchs. Vv 6-8 reports a second divine message, which structurally parallels the first in vv 1-5. Both contain: an introduction (vv 1, 6a); a command to an identified audience to hear the words of the covenant (vv 2, 6b); a curse against the one who does not keep the covenant (v 3) similar to the command to keep the covenant (v 6b); and a statement regarding the divine covenant with the patriarchs in both cases introduced by a causal conjunction (vv 4, 7). The first oracle concludes with prophetic assent (v 5b) while the second closes with the divine assessment of the people's refusal to keep the covenant. The parallelism between vv 1-5 and 6-8 perhaps was the basis for the expansion of vv 7-8, whose various parts have close parallels in other Deuteronomistic passages in Jeremiah (Thiel 1973:150-51; Tov 1972:196). After a brief introduction, vv 9-10 elaborate both the sin and judgement announced in vv 1-8. Like vv 1-8, this unit names Jerusalem and the inhabitants of Judah as culprits and disclaims the sins of their "first fathers," perhaps evoking like vv 1-8 the early "fathers" of Israel. Vv 11-12 announce judgement with the introduction formula *lākēn kōh ʾāmar yhwh*; elsewhere this formula of introducing judgement appears at the end of short prophetic oracles with a regular order of introduction, citation of fault and judgement. This unit thus builds on the preceding eleven verses. The *kî* clause of v 13 gives a further reason for the sin of Judah. The first half of this piece is paralleled in Jer 2:28b where the context more closely matches the topic of condemnation (McKane 1986:lvii, 243-44). The second half of v 13 continues with similar polemical material. The final verse, v 14, presents an injunction to Jeremiah to desist from intercession on the people's behalf (Seitz 1989a). In its present context, this order is a result of the massive sin of the people and reflects the irreversibility of the judgements proclaimed in the prior verses. This verse is tied to the prior units with the leitmotif of "hearing," *šmʿ* (11:2, 3, 7, 8, 10), but turns it on its head: because the people did not listen to Yahweh, now Yahweh will not listen to the people. The theme of the people's "evil" (*rāʿâ*) likewise connects v 14 to the preceding units (vv 8, 11, 12, 14) with the same reversal of theme: because of the people's evil (v 8), Yahweh will bring evil upon the people (vv 11, 12, 14).

Jer 11:15-16 is a poetic piece which lacks an introduction:

mh lydydy bbyty	What does my beloved want in my house?
ʿśwth hmzmth	Her doing is evil.
hrbym wbśr-qdš	The multitudes with holy flesh,
yʿbrw mʿlyk rʿtky	They would turn from you your evil;
ʾz tʿlzy	Then you would rejoice.
zyt rʿnn	"Luxuriant olive tree,
yph pry tʾr	With fruit beautiful in shape,"
qrʾ yhwh šmk	Yahweh named you.

lqwl hmwlh gdlh   With loud boisterous noise,
hṣyt ʾš ʿlyh   He has set it on fire
wrʿw dlywtyw   And its branches are broken.

Notes to Jer 11:15-16
It is possible to retain *hărabbîm* as subject of *yaʿabrû* and to view the waw prefixed on *ûbĕśar-qōdeš* as pleonastic (see Pope 1953). Most commentators take *kî* as a dittography (see Hyatt 1941:58). The last line of v 15 has been understood as a gloss (for radical surgery on these two verses with little or no textual support, see Hyatt 1941:59; cf. Wilhelmi 1975), but it suits what can be understood of the context. Its brevity would suggest an incongruity with its setting. The poetry of v 15 is not particularly parallelistic, but this verse may be understood as an example of the "prose-poetry" found sometimes in this book. For v 16a, Hyatt (1941:58) would delete *yhwh* since Yahweh is the speaker of the line and because the line is too long with the tetragrammaton; neither point is compelling.

The first line questions Yahweh's beloved in the temple. The use of the term, "beloved," reflects the sense of love — and perhaps now love lost — aimed by Yahweh toward "his beloved"; if so, an element of lament (which appears more explicitly in 12:7) may be implicit in this designation. The second line implies a negative answer in mentioning her sin. The third and fourth lines, if they are textually sound, refer to temple sacrifice (cf. Ps 65:3), which according to the fifth line, causes Jerusalem to exult. NJB takes the last three lines as a question in order to resolve the statement of a contrary to fact condition; that is, sacrifice will not, in fact, avert the judgement against Jerusalem. Verse 16 recalls the glory of Jerusalem as the tree with its beautiful fruit, presumably the people that grew from the cultic life of the temple (cf. *zayit raʿănān* in Ps 52:10). This recollection of Yahweh serves as a foil for the description of Jerusalem's destruction, presented as a past event.

Jer 11:15-16 is tied secondarily through a number of *Stichworte* and themes to the preceding and following prose pieces (11:17). McKane (1986:lxiv; cf. O'Connor 1988:105) suggests that v 17 represents a comment on v 15. The condemnation of making "incense to the baal" in 11:13 is continued in 11:17, which links the poetic unit of 11:14-17 with the prose section 11:1-13. Jerusalem and Judah are "summoned" **qrʾ* (11:6, 14, 15) to account for their "doing" (**ʿśh*) actions contrary to the divine will (11:8, 15) branded as "evil," **rāʿâ* (11:14, 15, 17). This will result in the destruction of Yahweh's "house," *bêt* (11:10, 15, 17). The image of the "house" (*bêt*) refers to Israel and Judah in 11:10 and 11:17, but 11:15 plays on the word, "house," in condemning the pollution of the divine house by the house of Israel and Judah. The verb, "to call" (*qrʾ*) in 11:14 and 16 illustrates the turn in the relationship between Yahweh and the people. In verse 14 Yahweh tells the prophet that Yahweh will not listen when the people "call to me." In part due to the wordplay between *rāʿâ*, *raʿănān* and *wěrāʿû* (v 16a, c), the image of the tree gives unity to this nexus of words: *zayit raʿănān* is the house which merits *rāʿâ* from the hand of Yahweh, and this destruction includes the breaking (*wěrāʿû*) of the tree's branches. Other connections with the following prose verse (11:17) include the image of the tree, the phrase *ʿlyk rʿh* (vv 15, 17) and perhaps the phonological resemblance between *hiṣṣît* (v 16) and *ṣěbāʾôt* (v 17). These connections between vv 15-16 and 17 partake of a further set of connecting words with the first lament in 11:18-20: the image of the tree (vv 16, 20); the preposition *ʿal* (vv 15, 17, 19) with the further pun on *maʿallêhem* (v 18); and perhaps the verbal resemblance of *biglal* (v 17) to *gillîtî* (v 20). Perhaps the phonological similarities between *dāliyyôtāyw* (v 16) and *kělāyôt* (v 20) also tie vv 15-16 to the first lament. The four units, 11:1-4, 15-16, 17, and 18-20, differ strongly in form and they lack formal relations. (Indeed, the unit of v 17 may have been prefixed to vv 18-20 under the implicit assumption that the first lament represented a prose unit.) The thematic and verbal connections serve to bridge the differences and provide a perspective on the events of Israel's existence; the first lament becomes a vehicle for expressing the need for judgement. More precisely, it exemplifies the reason for judgement.

The laments in 11:18-20 and 12:1-4 contain some of the *Stichworte* contained in the previous units and the themes which they embody (O'Connor 1988:106). For example, the judgement on the house of Israel and Judah (*bêt*) in 11:10 reverberates in 11:15, 17, and 12:6, 7. The leitmotif of "evil" (*rāʿâ*) punctuates 11:1-12:4. The word appears in vv 12, 14, 15, is then interrupted with puns in v 16 on *zayit raʿănān*, "verdant olive tree" (NJPS) and *wěrāʿû*, "they will break," and finally is picked up again in vv 22-23. The verbal connection of the tree with evil perhaps provides an interpretive clue also to the tree in the two laments: the tree is ultimately the evil people. The second and third divine speeches in 11-12 occur at the end of the unit.

The poetic words of 12:7-12 + 13 serve as a second divine response added to the first divine response of 12:5-6; v 13 may be linked secondarily to vv 7-12 through the similar words *nahălâ* and *nehlû*. Like 12:6, 12:8 depicts the speech of the prophet's enemies. Language of lamentation occurs in 12:4; the same case might be made for 12:7-13, at least insofar as elements of lament appear especially in vv 7-8 (M. S. Smith 1987b:97).

Certainly the image of the mourning land appears in 12:4 and 11. Jer 12:7-13 provides a second explanation of Israel's demise, beyond the announcement of judgement in 11:1-13. This unit does not present the problem simply as an issue of Israel's faithlessness to the covenant. Rather, the unit presents the problem in a more affective way: "she has lifted up her voice against me." Furthermore, the destruction by Yahweh is only secondary to the destruction brought by Israel's own shepherds.

Read in its larger context, the unit assumes further meaning. It suggests that Yahweh is innocent against the shepherds, *rōʿîm*, whose character is evoked by the phonologically similar occurrences of **rāʿâ* and the words with which it puns in 11:14-17 and 12:4. In other words, the evil, *rāʿâ*, visited upon Israel is to be blamed on Israel's shepherds, *rōʿîm*. By a similar repetition, the themes of 11:15-16 strike a chord in 12:7-13. In vv 15-16, Yahweh asks about *lîdîdî bēbêtî*, and the opening verse of 12:7-13 offers a divine lament to *bêtî//yĕdīdût napšî*. This conspicuous repetition perhaps implies a structural frame for the two laments. Other lexical items linking the two units, 11:15-16 and 12:7-13, could be marshalled as further support for this hypothesis (e.g., **bāśār* in 11:15 and 12:12; **rabbîm* in 11:15 and 12:10), but the items are too common to demonstrate such a claim. The argument of Diamond (1987:153, 156) that the divine pain expressed in 12:7-13 parallels the prophetic experience conveyed in the preceding prophetic lament would comport with the structural observation that the two divine speeches frame the two laments.

Like 19:17-27, 12:14-17 is an addition regarding the re-establishment in the land (see McKane 1986:lxiv). Furthermore, both 12:14-17 and 19:17-27 follow the lament at the end of a major section. The theme of portion (*naḥălātî*) in 12:7 resumes in verses 13-14. Jer 12:7 proclaims the divine abandonment of the *naḥălâ* of Israel; 12:13-14 reverses the theme, by announcing the restoration of the divine *naḥălâ*. Similarly, the theme of the land (*ʾereṣ*) threads its way from the second lament onward. It is picked up from the laments (11:19; 12:4) and in the divine response (12:5); moreover, the land is desolate in 12:7, but in 12:14, the land will be freed of its evil neighbors. Two motifs in this unit recall phrases in the initial speech of 11:1-14. The phrase, *bêt yĕhûdâ*, in 12:14 not only takes up the theme of *bêt* in 11:14-17 and 12:4; it also evokes the longer forms *bêt-yiśrāʾēl ûbêt yĕhûdâ* in 11:10. Similarly, the theme of swearing appearing in 12:16 serves to complement the original oath of Yahweh to the patriarchs mentioned in 11:5. If patterning is to be read from the parallels of "house" in 11:10 and 12:4, and oaths in 11:5 and 12:6, and from other parallels between the two units, 11:15-16 and 12:7-13, it might be argued that the structure of introductory prose piece plus lament has been modified secondarily to be understood in the following way:

A   Introductory prose judgement: 11:1-14
B   Divine poetic lament announcing judgement: 11:15-17
C   Lament plus response: 11:18-23
C' Lament plus response: 12:1-6
B' Divine poetic lament announcing judgement: 12:7-13
A' Introductory prose judgement: 12:14-17

If this arrangement were correct, the judgements are designed to be read with a number of modifications. First, the prophet's fate stands as a central example of the difficulties in the relationship between Yahweh and Israel. Second, the placement of the two divine pieces in 11:15-16 and 12:7-13 around the two prophetic laments emphasizes how treatment of the prophet parallels the treatment of Yahweh at the hands of Israel (Diamond 1987:153, 156; M. S. Smith 1987b:98): both the prophet and the deity desired to benefit Israel, and both were attacked by Israel. Third, judgement remains the fate of Israel despite these exigencies. Finally, this interpretation in the modification of chapters 11-12 would explain why this major unit juxtaposes two laments.

To summarize the divine speeches in 11-12, these chapters have, relative to the other units in chapters 11-20, little material added apart from the introductory prose judgement and the divine response following the laments in 11:18-23 and 12:1-6. More precisely, chapters 11-12 contain three additions besides introductory prose composition and the prophetic laments. The first addition is 11:15-17, itself consisting of two units, vv 15-16 and v 17, which are divine speeches linked secondarily to the initial section of prose judgement. This section functions as part of the preceding prose condemnation. The second section is 12:7-13, which constitutes a second divine response to the laments, although in its present context it is designed to be read as part of 12:5-6. The third divine speech of the unit, 12:14-17, is a prose unit which closes chapters 11-12.

In sum, chapters 11-12 as a whole give the impression of a dialogue between Yahweh and Jeremiah, embodied first in the two laments and their divine responses, and the enveloping of those pieces by further divine speeches (cf. Diamond 1987:34). The love language expressed in the second divine response to the second lament places the problem of

judgement in an affective perspective which could provide solace to
Israel during and after the exile.

2. CHAPTERS 13-15

This unit is more complex than chapters 11-12, although like 11-12, it
includes the formation of introductory prose piece and prophetic lament.
The initial divine speech material follows on the heels of the introductory
prose judgement in 13:1-11. The superscription of v 1a is followed by a
short prophetic story, vv 1b-7 + 8-11 (McKane 1986:lxxii). The story includes a series of pronouncements of judgement in vv 9-11. The judgements of vv 9-10 take their departures from the verbs *nišḥat* and *yiṣlaḥ* in
v 7. The judgement in v 11 is less neatly connected to the story (it may be
secondary, joined loosely by the subordinating conjunction *kî* [cf. Jer
15:5]).

Jer 13:12-14 functions as a second symbol representing Israel's fate
(see McKane 1986:lxxii). The grouping of this material with 13:1-11 probably stemmed from the similarity of material (cf. 12:7-13 added as a second divine response to the prophetic lament): both units draw out a
symbol. The spoiled waistcloth, which serves as a sign of lost closeness
between Yahweh and Judah in 13:1-11, is followed by the wine jar sym-
bolizing Judah's drunkenness in 13:12-14. Both exemplify Israel's loss of
Yahweh and its impending destruction. V 14 more specifically involves
an additional message of judgement which does not play off one of the
two preceding symbols.

Following the announcement of judgement in the form of the two
symbols in 13:1-14, diverse poetic and prose material appears down to
the lament of Jeremiah beginning in 15:15 (some scholars, including
Diamond 1987:52-64 and O'Connor 1988:27-44, view 15:10 as the beginning of the lament). The unit of Jer 13:15-27 bears superficial signs of
connection with the preceding unit. The figure of Jerusalem in vv 9 and
27, and the expressions for divine speech in vv 14 and 15 connect the two
units. Jer 13:17 picks up the theme of "not listening" in 13:11, echoing the
theme of Judah's sin. Less clear connections include **yrd* in 13:11 and 18,
*yn in 13:11 and 20, and perhaps the phonetic resemblance between *gĕʾôn*
in 13:9 and *gēbâ* in 13:17.

The material from 13:15 to 15:9 gives the impression of a conversation among a variety of interlocutors (cf. Diamond 1987:63, 158, 161). In

the first set of material, 13:15-14:10, there are three parts: (1) poetic judgement in 13:15-27 (itself a complex of various material; Overholt 1988:621); (2) the lament of the people in 14:1-9;[1] and (3) poetic judgement in 14:10. The first part presents Yahweh announcing judgement against Israel. In the second part Israel laments to Yahweh. Yahweh remains steadfast in judgement in the third part.

The second group of material runs from 14:11 to 14:16. This section is considerably shorter than either the preceding or following cycle. Like the first section, 14:11-12 opens with a message of judgement against Israel. It is followed by a brief word by Jeremiah in 14:13, and judgement is announced again in 14:14-16. Like the previous section, this one gives an impression of a dialogue, this time between Yahweh and the prophet. Finally, the third cycle of material in 14:17-15:9 offers a judgement in 14:17-18. Connected to 14:17-18 by the theme of "being smitten," the people's lament follows in 14:19-22 and judgement is reiterated in 15:1-9 (a diverse group of material, linked secondarily in MT by *kî* in v 5; Diamond 1987:159). The theme of famine as judgement appears in all three parts of this section (Holladay 1986:422; for the view that 14:17-21 generated 15:1-4, see McKane 1986:lxvi).

All three groups of material bear a symmetry, creating the impression of a dialogue. In the first and third group, two divine judgements flank a human response to judgement. In the second cycle, Jeremiah's word appears in the middle, in 14:10, flanked by the words of the people. Finally, it may be observed that the laments in 15:10-21 appear as another dialogue. Built on the model of the basic lament form of human complaint and divine answer, the two laments function as a dialogue between Yahweh and Jeremiah. Jeremiah laments his birth in 15:10, and Yahweh responds with judgement against Israel in 15:11-14. Jeremiah begins a lament in 15:15, which Yahweh answers in 15:18-21.

Some themes punctuate chapters 13-15. The word, "name," appears toward various ends in different settings: 13:11; 14:9, 15, 21; and 15:16. It connects the fate of Jeremiah with the people and the false prophets, as all three groups make a claim on the divine name. The question of prophecy and its efficacy also appears in this unit, specifically in 14:17, 19, and 15:18. Holladay's emphasis (1986:422; O'Connor 1987:107) on the theme of mother in chapters 14-15 is highly suggestive. It would appear that this theme extends to chapter 13 as well and provides a basis for thematic continuity over the highly diverse material in these chapters. It

---

[1] For the image of Jer 14:4, cf. KTU 1.16 III, especially line 12.

may be related to other female images for Jerusalem: her title, *hārabbâ, [2] in 13:9; prostitute in 13:22b, 26-27; the lamenting Jerusalem in 14:2; and "the virgin daughter of my people," bĕtûlat bat-ʿammî, in 14:17 (Fitzgerald 1975:174 n. 19). The maternal theme appears initially in this major section in 13:21 where Jerusalem is called ʾēšet lēdâ, "a birthing mother." This image relates to the description of the impending widowhood of the people in 15:7-9 and Jeremiah's mother giving birth to him in his sustained curse of 15:10-14. This correspondence may imply more: the life of Jeremiah has a paradigmatic quality. Jerusalem's children are cursed like Jeremiah; the fate of the people thus corresponds to the fate of the prophet. Indeed, the evocation of widowhood in 15:7-9 introduces and connects 14:1-15:9 to the curse of 15:10-14. Other phrases also link the unit of 15:5-9 to 15:10-14: ûšěʾērîtām, "and their remnant," in 15:9 and "your remnant," šērûtěkā (ketib) (cf. šērîtîkā [qere]) in 15:11; *ʾōyēb, "enemy" in 15:9, 11, 14; and the parallel phrases, "to the sword I will give," laḥereb ʾetēn, in v 9, and "for plunder I will give," lābaz ʾetēn, in v 13.

Furthermore, Jeremiah's lament in 15:15-21 is related by its context to the fate of the people. This thrust is made explicit by the parallelism of the people's lament in 14:7-9 and the prophet's lament in 15:15-21. That the two are related is clear from wěšimkā ʿālênû niqrāʾ in 14:9 and niqrāʾ

---

[2] The word hārāb appears to be haplography of the final hê thanks to the following hāʿām (as many commentators have suggested); read *hārabbâ. The epithet of rabbâ (and the older Northwest Semitic forms with final feminine ending -t) is commonly applied to cities in West Semitic texts; the masculine form does not occur otherwise (for Mesopotamian use of the masculine form of the same root with cities, see Fisher 1963:35-36). Fitzgerald (1972:407) lists the following examples of the feminine epithet, "great one," applied to cities:

(1) rbt bny ʿmwn (Deut 3:11); rbh (Josh 13:25)

(2) sydwn rbh (Josh 11:8; 19:28)

(3) ʾudm rbt ʾudm ṯrrt (KTU 1.14 II 5-6, III 30, IV 47-48, V 41-42 [reconstructed], VI 11-12)

(4) ḫbr rbt ḫbr ṯrrt (KTU 1.15 IV 8-9, 19-20, V 25-26)

(5) ḳʿyr rbty...rbty (Lam 1:1)

(6) ṣur-riʾāl rabitu (EA 147:62)

To the list of Ugaritic examples may be added the names, ʾaršḫ rbt wʾaršḫ ṯrrt (KTU 1.100.63-64), probably two place-names named after the Tigris (ʾaršḫ being the Hurrian name for the Tigris). On this interpretation, see Pardee 1988:215; cf. de Moor 1987:153 n. 26.

šimkā ʿālay in 15:16 (cf. *šimkā* in 14:21). The wound (**makkâ*) of both the people (14:17) and the prophet (15:19) likewise links the presentation of the prophet in lament with the rendering of the people in lament. The use of questions in both laments (14:18-19; 15:18) also connects the two laments. The prophetic lament read in conjunction with the people's lament also emphasizes judgement against the people. Indeed, reading the prophetic lament in this manner has the force of identifying the people as Jeremiah's enemies. Judgement against the people is reinforced by the relationship between 15:11-14 and the prophetic lament following in 15:15-18. There are verbal connections between 15:11-14 and 15:15-18: **ydʿ*, "to know," in 15:14 and 15; divine "anger," **ʾap*, in vv 14 and 15; and perhaps the verbal sequence, *qādĕḥâ* (v 14)...*tûqād* (v 14)...*ûpāqĕdēnî* (v 15). These verbal connections translate into thematic ones: Jeremiah prays for deliverance from the divine wrath coming against the people.

3. CHAPTERS 16-17

The various material from 16:1-17:13 is highly diverse. Nonetheless, it shows some signs of a patterned arrangement with a theological purpose.

In its present form, 16:14-18 belongs with 16:1-13 (for the complexity of the material and their relations, see McKane 1986:lxxii-lxxiii, 368-79). Jer 16:14-15 is an addition designed to temper the judgement announced in 16:13, 16-18. These two verses are connected to the preceding unit through the theme of the "fathers" in 16:12, and land in 16:13, 15, 18.

Jer 16:19-21 appears to be a piece presenting a dialogue between Yahweh and the nations. The themes of fathers (16:11, 12, 19) and false gods (16:13, 20) connect this piece to the preceding unit. In this unit the nations function as a foil to Israel; the nations are presented as recognizing Yahweh in contrast to Israel's failing to acknowledge Yahweh. This contrast leads to the condemnation of Judah in 17:1-4 (knowledge occurring also in 16:21 and 17:1).[3] This passage is secondarily connected to

---

[3] The word *zkr* in v 2 poses some difficulty. NAB, NJPS and RSV translate with MT pointing as an infinitive meaning, "to remember" (so also Carroll 1986:348; McKane 1986:384; cf. Holladay 1986:484). NJPS recognizes in a note the meaning "memorial." The old Jewish Publication Society translation renders the word as a noun, "the symbols," evidently abandoning the MT vocalization. Similarly, Volz (1922:184) read the word as *zikkārôn*, "a memorial stele." The root **zkr* refers to the

16:1-18 by the word *naḥălâ*, "portion" which appears in 16:18 and 17:4. Like 16:1-18, 17:1-4 announces judgement against the people. Finally, "double-sin" in 16:18 anticipates the "double-destruction" voiced by the prophet in his lament in 17:18. Hence the parallels between the two passages, 16:1-18 and 17:1-4, link the judgement voiced by Yahweh and the prophet, and the prophetic trials voiced in the lament becomes paradigmatic for the nation at large.

17:5-11 contains a collection of proverbial material. Like Psalm 1, this material divides people into two types. The connections with 17:1-4 include the image of the tree (17:2, 6-8; cf. fruit in v 10), the reference to the heart (17:1, 5) and the description of the land. The image of the heart is a forceful one in 17:1, 5 and 10; in each case, the heart is the location of personal posture toward Yahweh. The verb ʿzb, "to forsake" in 17:11 and 13 links the loss of riches by the one who gains them wrongfully with the one who abandons Yahweh (Carroll 1986:359; O'Connor 1988:108). Perhaps the repetition of the verb suggests an analogy of unrighteous behavior; indeed, 17:11 presents precisely this sort of analogy. The image of water in 17:8 and 13 points to Yahweh as the source of living waters and the necessity of the people to draw on these waters (Carroll 1986:353). There is an interesting pun further linking 17:5-11 with 17:16.

---

function of memorial in a number of Northwest Semitic texts. According to 2 Sam 18:18, Absalom erects a stele, because he has no son to "invoke" (*zkr) his name (cf. Isa 56:3; 66:3; KAI 214:16, 21). A Hellenistic period Phoenician inscription from the environs of Athens, KAI 53, attests the practice of erecting a memorial stele (*mṣbt*) as a memorial (*śkr*, cognate with *zkr). This funerary practice is attested also in both Ugaritic (KTU 1.17 I 28; 6.13; 6.14) and Mesopotamian texts (see *šuma zakāru* in CAD E, 400a; Z, 18). In these instances the memorial stele was dedicated by sons in honor of their fathers' memory. This view applied to Jer 17:2 may account for *zkr (possibly a qitl nominal formation), standing in construct to *bĕnêhem*. The phrase *zkr bĕnêhem* corresponds to *waʾăšērîm* in the next line just as *mizbĕḥôtām* corresponds to *ʿal-ʿēṣ raʿănān*. Both of these images may be viewed as analogues to illustrate the point of the preceding verse, namely how near sin is to Judah. The two images therefore both are employed to convey proximity; in this case *mizbĕḥôtām* would constitute an adverbial accusative. The following translation may be then suitable (on the difficulty of the final line, see Propp 1987:231):

> ...like their sons' memorial by their altars,
> and their asherim by the luxuriant tree,
> on the highest hills.

If the nominal rendering of *zkr cannot be sustained, it might be argued nonetheless that the infinitival form refers to the custom of commemorating parents.

The heart that is incurable or sickly, *ʾānūš*," in 17:9 is echoed in the day that is called *ʾānûš*, understood as a "day of disaster" in 17:16. This is an unparalleled expression for a day (Diamond 1987:242 n. 27), and the verbal echo seems deliberate. Another interesting poetic connection between the two sections is made by two temporal phrases. The word, *ûbĕʾaḥărîtô* in verse 11, understood as "in the end," seems to constitute a natural bond with *mērîʾšôn* in verse 12, rendered "as of old" (NJPS). Together the two words form a semantic word-pair,[4] perhaps providing a secondary connection between the two units.

The unit, 17:12-13, presents a short prayer by the people. It is connected not only with the previous unit, but with 17:1-11 as a whole. It shares two striking notes with the opening section of chapter 17. The themes of the sanctuary (17:1, 12) and the fate written (17:1, 13) give a measure of cohesion to 17:1-13 as a unit. The passage also illustrates that the people do not even know how they have so misunderstood the status of the temple and their written fate. While the people regard the temple as a sign of security (17:12), it is now in Yahweh's eyes a place polluted by the people's deeds (17:1). While the people acknowledge the fate of those who "are written in the earth" (17:13), a phrase expressing condemnation to death, it is the people themselves who bear this fate (17:1). Finally, the shame in 17:13 is recognized and condemned by the people, but the prophet proclaims in 17:18 that it is their own shame; it implies their eventual condemnation.

Jer 17:19-27 is an addition confirming the iniquity of the people (cf. McKane 1986:lxxiii-lxxiv). A number of commentators (Carroll 1986:368; Holladay 1986:509; McKane 1986:417-18; cf. Overholt 1988:623) view the unit as post-exilic (see Introduction). This unit may have been attracted to its present position by virtue of the same type of story following in 18:1-11, just as 12:7-13 was added as a second divine response and 13:12-14 was inserted as a second symbol.

The material in chapters 16-17 presents the ambiguity of Judah's situation from the human point of view and the clarity of the same situation from the divine perspective. The people recognize the traditional marks of sin and the traditional explanations for it, but they do not see that it is their own sin. From the divine perspective, there is no ambiguity, since Yahweh sees into the human heart and knows. This discourse on human nature, as it applies to Judah, sets the stage for the prophetic

---

[4] Avishur 1984 does not include this pair in his analysis of BH word-pairs. However, cf. Deut 11:12; Eccles 7:8.

lament in 17:14-18. The two sections are connected secondarily through grammatical means. The nearest antecedent for "they" in v 15 is those who "have forsaken the source of the water of life — Yahweh" in v 13. Therefore the prophet's discourse against the enemies in his lament applies secondarily to the people discussed in the previous section. As with the contexts of other laments, this one has the force of identifying the people as Jeremiah's enemies who are therefore subject to Yahweh's judgement. The section following in 17:19-27 perhaps provides an illustration of the people's sin.

4. CHAPTERS 18-20

The pattern of introductory story plus lament appears in a unique fashion in this section, since it has been duplicated. The potter stories of 18:1-11 and 19:1-13 constitute the initial units of two parallel subsections which end in a prophetic lament (Thiel 1973:161-62, 228-29; Diamond 1987:172). This may be viewed in the following manner:

A   18:1-11   prose judgement in potter story
B   18:19-23   prophetic lament
A'   19:1-15   prose judgement in potter story
B'   20:7-18   prophetic lament

As this schema illustrates, chapters 18-20 twice present the structure of prose judgement plus prophetic lament.

The material added to the basic pattern of introductory story plus prophetic lament within chapters 18-20 is 18:13-18, and 20:1-6 and 14-18. Jer 18:13-18 is linked to 18:1-12 by various verbal elements: *nt*š in vv 7 and 14; *šěrîrût* in v 12 and *ša'ărûrît* in v 13; and perhaps the phonetic resemblance between *hayyôṣēr* in vv 3, 4, and 6 and *miṣṣûr* in v 14. Jer 20:1-6 is a prose piece connected to 19:15 only by common words, namely *šm'* "to hear," and *dābār*, "matter, word." Jer 20:1-6 is also connected to the lament of 20:7-13 explicitly through the image of "terror surrounding" (*māgôr missābîb*) in 20:3, 10 and by the issue of prophecy in 20:6, 9.

The unit of 18:12 + 13-18 reflects a structure opposite to the cycles of speeches in chapters 13-15. In 18:12 the people reject the word of Yahweh, positionally represented by the preceding 18:1-11. The rejection of Yahweh's message in 18:12 is followed by a poetic section of divine judgement in 18:13-17. The verbal connection between 18:12 and 18:13-17 comes in the form of a pun: *šĕrīrût*, "stubbornness" (RSV) or "willfulness" (NJPS) in 18:12 and *šaʿărūrīt*, "horrible thing" (RSV and NJPS) in 18:13 (Diamond 1987:170). The people declare their own willfulness in 18:12 and the divine judgement opens with the question of who has ever heard of such a horrible thing. Indeed, this choice in Israel's path is called twice in 18:15 "going in their own way," a phrase echoing 18:11. The judgement of 18:17 declares Israel's destruction. Yahweh will give Israel his *ʿōrep*, elsewhere the neck (an image perhaps playing on the people's stiff-necked rejection of Yahweh's ways in 19:15).

Diamond (1987:172) and Fretheim (1987:64) observe the correspondence between Yahweh and Jeremiah drawn by 18:12 and 18:18. Diamond emphasizes that the people's refusal to repent in v 12 parallels their rejection of the prophet's mission in v 18. Fretheim stresses how the people's plans (*maḥšĕbôt*) against Yahweh in v 12 parallel their plots (*maḥăšābôt*) against Jeremiah in v 18. With their rejection of Yahweh comes their rejection of Yahweh's prophet. Moreover, Fretheim points out that judgement follows both instances of this root, conveying the idea that Jeremiah's cry for vengeance corresponds to the divine announcement of judgement. Hence, the word rejected by the people in Jer 18:18 comes in the form of a rejection of Yahweh's messenger. This second rejection leads into the prophetic lament of 18:19-23 and provides the theological context for this lament.

Jer 18:12-18 constitutes three parts in a dialogue between Yahweh and the people, like the first and third cycles of material in chapters 13-15. Yet, 18:12-18 turns this structure inside out. In this unit, the divine word stands between the two pieces quoting the people's rejection of this word. Whereas the people's words in chapters 13-15 constitute prayer, the people's words in 18:12-18 constitute condemnation of Yahweh's word. The people thereby confirm their own condemnation. With the rejection of God's word, the condemnation of Judah is presented as irreversible and deserved. Indeed, the preceding sermon in 18:1-11 provides the explicit guide to interpreting this series of speeches. In 18:11 Yahweh announces the divine "scheme" (*ḥšb*), i.e. judgement against Israel. The people's words in 18:12 include their intention to follow their own "schemes," seen in v 18 to be their "scheme" against the prophet. Hence the scheme of the people in the lament becomes paradigmatic for the sin which provokes Yahweh's judgement.

Jer 18:13-17 is related to 18:18 + 19-23 in a number of ways which orient the meaning of the prophetic lament in vv 19-23. In its present setting, the suffixed forms of "them" of v 17 (-ēm and -ām) serve as the antecedent for wayyōʾmĕrû in v 18. In this way the two passages are made to have the same referent. The root *kšl, "to stumble," appears in vv 15 and 23, which thus applies to the same people. The unnamed enemies of the prophet's lament in vv 19-23 encompass the enemies of Yahweh in vv 13-17. The use of *ḥšb, "to scheme" in vv 11, 12 and 18 (O'Connor 1988:109) has the similar effect of tying the introductory prose piece to the lament. These interconnections harmonize the referents and topics among the various pieces in chapter 18.

The prose stories of chapters 19-20 are likewise connected to the lament in 20:7-13. The form lōʾ-yûkal in 19:11 connects to wĕlōʾ ʾûkāl in 20:9 and other combinations on the letters /k/ and /l/ in this lament. (Does the reference to the tophet in 19:12-13 link chapter 19 to the lament through the reference to the prophet's bones in 20:9?) The referent of māgôr missābîb in 20:10 is provided in 20:3 (O'Connor 1988:111). While this phrase in the lament represents a quoted phrase, it assumes a personal identification in the preceding prose narrative. This phrase which describes the prophet's situation in the lament acquires a concrete referent in the prose story. Common roots, such as *šēm, "name" (20:3, 9) and *rʾh, "to see" (20:4, 12) represent less forceful connections between 20:1-6 and 7-13.

There is one further section within chapters 18-20 which has a significant bearing on the laments in this section. The final section of chapters 11-20, Jer 20:14-18, discloses a further purpose relative to the laments. It has been argued that this passage represents the last of the prophetic laments. However, as stated in chapter one, there are reasons against viewing the section as a lament. Jer 20:14-18 resembles rather the curses of Jer 15:10-15 and Job 3 (O'Connor 1988:78; Parker 1988):

(14)   Cursed be the day I was born!
        The day my mother bore me,
        Let it not be blessed!

(15)   Curse be the man who gave my father the news,
        "A son is born to you,"
        Making him very joyful.

(16)   Let that man be like the cities
        Which Yahweh overthrew without pity;
        May he hear a cry in the morning,
        And a battle alarm at noon,

(17)   Because he did not kill me in the womb,
        So that my mother might be my grave,
        And her womb forever big.
(18)   Why did I come of the womb,
        To see misery and woe,
        And spend (*klh) my days in shame?[5]

The prophet curses his life by cursing the event of his origins. He prays that he remain in his mother's womb so that she be large with him, never having emerged. The curse of this section is elaborate compared with the parallel in Job 3. As Parker (1988:134-35, 139-42) observes, 20:14-15 has three distinctive features compared to other examples of the topos of the birth-announcement: (a) the addition of the term, zākār, "male," after bēn, "son"; (b) the mention of the theme of joy, not mentioned in other biblical examples of the motif of the birth announcement (but appearing in one Ugaritic instance, KTU 1.10 III); and (c) the more prosaic character of the passage. The three elements draw out the sheer weight which the prophet expresses over his life. Vv 15-17 elaborate the cursing of the announcer of the prophet's birth. The emphasis on the curse, special to this instance of the birth-announcement, may be traced to the specific context of Jeremiah's own life. On one level, this passage curses the circumstance of Jeremiah's birth; on another level, 20:15-16 curses the messenger of his birth, which evokes the prophet's own present circumstances. Jeremiah is, after all, a prophet called from birth (Jer 1:5).

If Jer 20:13 seems a high note, 20:18 is a low note. This final verse states that the prophet's days are "spent" in shame. The word "spent" evokes an important wordplay connecting this verse with the whole of the final lament in 20:7-13, a unit which uses the consonants /k/ and /l/ in a variety of formations (see chapter one, section six). Jeremiah's days *klh, "pass," in shame. The verbal root *klh resonates with the verb *ykl, "to be able," which frequently appears in the lament. Who was "able" in the end? The final word in 20:18 leaves the audience with the sense that there is yet no victory for the prophet. Although the last lament leaves the audience on a positive note, the conclusion to the laments in 20:14-18,

---

[5] For the use of 'ăšer in v 17 in the meaning of "because," see MacDonald 1975:167, who takes this usage as an indication of spoken Hebrew as opposed to written Hebrew. For the lack of mappiq in raḥmāh in v 17, see Joüon 94h. For other interpretations of this word, see McKane 1986:489.

indeed to the whole of chapters 11-20, establishes the tension between deliverance and destruction.

FOUR

⚜

Concluding Remarks

1. THE THEODICY OF THE DIVINE SPEECHES

The divine speeches in Jeremiah 11-20 exhibit some progression of thought and action. In chapters 11-12 God's affection for Israel is seen to have been violated by Israel. This initial situation presupposes God's affection for Israel, a state of affairs indicated by Yahweh's title for Israel of *yĕdîd*, "beloved." In chapters 13-15 Israel's actions against Yahweh are addressed. In this unit, Yahweh expresses divine affection for Israel, and stands in dialogue with Israel. In pronouncing judgement, Yahweh elicits a response from the people, one of lament for their fate. Yet this intention appears insufficient. In this section, Yahweh has listened. In chapters 16-17 a divine meditation on trust appears at center-stage; this piece presents a standard for assessing the heart of each person. The text does not resolve the tension over the referent of the wisdom piece. The referent of the wisdom piece is left unstated; perhaps 17:19-27 may be designed to answer this tension — it is the people who do not trust in Yahweh. Like chapters 13-15, chapters 18-20 present a dialogue between Yahweh and the people. But the dialogue in this case does not include the people's prayer; rather, the note sounded by the people is rejection of Yahweh. Although Yahweh has spoken through the prophet and expressed clear standards of behavior both in prophetic and wisdom terms, the laments of the people of the second unit are replaced in the fourth unit by their condemnation of Yahweh. The necessity of the exile is evident.

The relationship between Yahweh and Jeremiah serves as a vehicle for expressing the breakdown in the relationship between Yahweh and Israel. More specifically, one function of the divine speeches is to focus on the relationship between Yahweh and Jeremiah to the exclusion of the people or enemies, and this feature is consistent with other material within chapters 11-20. Jeremiah 11-20 departs from what might be expected from a prophetic book. Unlike most prophetic material which presents a prophet delivering the divine word to the people, Jeremiah 11-20 presents speeches by the prophet and Yahweh delivered not only to the people, but to one another. Within the material the people mostly remain outside the dialogue, except as a topic of conversation. The voice of the people is heard during the dialogue between Yahweh and Jeremiah. Yet, this voice comes second-hand to the audience. Mediated by the framework of the dialogue between Yahweh and Jeremiah, the voice of the enemies emerges from the background and is not immediately present to the audience. Likewise, the divine prohibition on Jeremiah's prophesying in 11:14 and 14:11 (Wilson 1980:238; O'Connor 1988:131-32 n. 63) creates a setting that literarily sets Jeremiah and Yahweh before the audience and leaves the people in the background. This modification in the customary prophetic format offers an alternative way of presenting the divine word to the audience.[1] Within the context of the divine speeches, the laments with their human complaints and divine responses become part of the portrait of the special relationship between Jeremiah and Yahweh.

This identification between prophet and deity, sometimes at the exclusion of the people, is made also through explicit assertions. Three specific examples of identification between the prophet and his deity may be noted. First, there are statements of formal relationship between Yahweh and Jeremiah. In 15:20 Yahweh says to Jeremiah that "I am with you to save you and deliver you." Secondly, Jeremiah laments about his enemies in 11:20, and then he asks Yahweh that they be seen as the enemies of Yahweh as well (12:3). Thirdly, following a divine word describing divine anger (15:14; cf. 10:10, 24-25; 12:13; 18:23), the third lament reverses the traditional function of prophecy. God fills Jeremiah not with

[1] An exclusion of the audience would provide evidence that the audience intended for chapters 11-20 as a whole is not an audience mentioned in the text. It would seem to suggest that a reading audience receiving a written form of prophecy is involved (for discussions presenting a comparable view of Ezekiel, see Loisy 1910:196; von Rad 1965:222-23; Wilson 1988b:657-58; Davis 1989; Darr 1989; for the written character of Second Isaiah, see Begrich 1938:93; Eissfeldt 1965:340; Wilson 1988a:60; cf. Gitay 1980). Writing as the medium for prophecy dates as early as the late eighth century, used either for proclamation (Hab 2:2) or storage (Isa 8:19-20). See also Isa 29:11-12; 30:11; Jer 25:13; 26. For literacy in ancient Israel, see Lemaire 1981; Crenshaw 1985; Millard 1987; Haran 1988.

sympathy for the people whom Jeremiah is called to serve as a mediating prophet. Rather, as Jeremiah says, "you have filled me with indignation" (15:17). The divine indignation becomes Jeremiah's anger.

Identification between Yahweh and Jeremiah also takes place on inexplicit levels insofar as both figures receive abuse from the people and call for judgement against the people. According to Diamond (1987:153, 156), the divine lament of 12:7-13 expresses the divine pain at the hands of the people, parallel to the prophetic experience conveyed in the preceding prophetic lament. As noted in chapter three, section four, Diamond (1987:172) and Fretheim (1987:64) observe the parallel between Yahweh and Jeremiah established by 18:12 and 18. Diamond emphasizes that refusal of the people to repent in v 12 parallels their rejection of the prophet's mission. Fretheim stresses how the people's plans (maḥšebôt) against Yahweh in v 12 parallel their plots (maḥăšābôt) against Jeremiah in v 18. The close relationship between Yahweh and Jeremiah and the disjunction between prophet and people highlight the distance between Yahweh and the people.

The dialogue between Yahweh and Jeremiah also qualifies the nature of judgement. The divine speeches not only present judgement; they also describe the character of the condemnation by providing it with an intelligible rationale. In at least one context, the divine discourse expresses judgement in affective terms. Jer 12:5-13, which forms a second divine response to the second lament of Jeremiah 12:1-4, evokes the love language known from Hosea 1-3 and elsewhere in Jeremiah (2:2-3; 3:1; cf. 3:12-14, 19-20). Jer 12:7-8 are the words of the divine lover:

(7)   I have forsaken my house,
        I have abandoned my heritage;
        I have given the beloved of my soul
        Into the hands of her enemies.

(8)   My heritage has become to me like a lion in the forest,
        She has lifted up her voice against me;
        Therefore I hate her.

This imagery is dramatic — the picture of the divine lover abandoning the beloved (cf. Heschel 1962:111).[2] While it utilizes love language known from prior prophetic tradition, this passage makes the further dramatic

---

[2] For ancient Near Eastern parallels, see Gwaltney 1983.

claim that Yahweh is the victim. The lion who roars is here not Yahweh (cf. Isa 31:4-9; Jer 25:30; Amos 1:2; 3:8; Joel 3:16); rather, it is Israel. Worse, it is against Yahweh that Israel roars (Holladay 1986:387). Here the rejected lover is Yahweh, a point reinforced by Jer 15:6: "You have rejected me." Yahweh is the one whom Israel has given up.[3] This example of divine love provides an important sub-theme to the larger context of theodicy. The suffering of Jeremiah is a dramatic symbol in the laments. Yet, beyond the pain of Jeremiah over Israel sent in exile lies the torment of the one who sent the prophet. The few examples of divine lament in Jeremiah make an affective appeal to the audience by exploring a side of Yahweh; these divine speeches provide an emotional picture of what happened in the early sixth century. The people rejected their source of life; then Judah fell, Jerusalem was besieged and burned, and its inhabitants were killed or exiled. The pain of Yahweh reflects a divine heart capable of mercy. Mercy will be possible when Yahweh, the spurned lover, is taken back again.

In summary, the divine speeches develop the meaning of the laments. Given the divine speeches and other material as their context, the laments partake of three purposes beyond the older function of defending the legitimacy of Jeremiah's prophetic vocation. The laments in context function to announce Yahweh's judgement against Israel, to show the people's fault and the impact of that sin on Yahweh as the spurned partner to the covenant, and finally, to present Jeremiah's special identification with Yahweh as sign and symbol of Israel's relationship with Yahweh. This third function is further evident from the larger context of the laments in the chapters surrounding Jeremiah 11-20.

2. THE LARGER CONTEXT OF THE LAMENTS

The context of the laments is not limited to the material in chapters 11-20. Motifs in chapters 11-20 extend beyond these boundaries (O'Connor 1988:118-47). A few points of comparison between chapters 11-20 and the chapters surrounding them illustrate some functions of the laments.

---

[3] Jer 9:7-11 similarly combines judgement with an emotional description of Yahweh (see M. S. Smith 1987b).

Chapters 11-20 reflect significant continuity with the preceding chapters in their depiction of the prophet's relationship with the people. O'Connor (1988:123-30) argues that chapters 2-10 present a conciliatory tone between Yahweh and the people while chapters 11-20 move to a more clearly articulated position of judgement. The temple sermon in chapter 7 bears out this view in part. Jer 7:16 forbids Jeremiah's intercession on behalf of the people; the distance between Yahweh and the people has become irreconciliable. Seitz (1989a:8-9; cf. Diamond 1987:153) suggests that chapters 1-6 mark the stage when the people's repentance is still acceptable to Yahweh and it is still possible to avoid divine punishment, whereas chapters 7-20 mark the end of divine patience and the beginning of divine wrath. The tone of sympathy in chapters 7-10 belongs less to Yahweh than to the prophet; chapters 11-20 mark the loss of the prophet's sympathetic identification with the people. In these chapters the prophet's posture parallels the divine disposition. The motif of the "hurt" within the two major units is compatible with this interpretation. Within chapters 7-10, specifically in 8:18, 21-22, and 10:19, the motif signals Jeremiah's identification with the people. In chapters 11-20, however, the hurt separates the prophet from the people (15:18; 17:14). In 11-20 the prophet cannot intercede despite this hurt; he witnesses to the hurt (11:14; 14:17; 15:1). Besides a reversal in theme, the motif of hurt also points to Jeremiah's relationship with Yahweh. Yahweh can heal the hurt of Jeremiah; it is too late for the people. Moreover, the unjust hurt is not one which the people suffers at God's hands (14:17), but one which Jeremiah suffers at the people's hands (cf. Diamond 1987:153,156).

Chapters 11-20 would appear to present an alteration in the relationship between Jeremiah and the people compared with chapters 7-10. While chapters 7-10 provide examples of the prophet's solidarity with the people, chapters 11-20 reflect the separation of the prophet from the people and emphasize rather his relationship with Yahweh. The shift between 7-10 and 11-20 raises a number of issues for the laments in Jeremiah 11-20. The changes in the motif of hurt perhaps point to the meaning of chapters 7-20 and the significance of the laments within this larger unit. The motif of hurt links the plight of the people with the plight of the prophet in 7-10. Then in 11-20 it reflects the distance between Jeremiah and the people over the understanding of God's will and plan.

One function of chapters 11-20 relative to 21-25 is to predispose the audience to the guilt of the enemies whose identity is discussed at great length in chapters 21-25.[4] As Diamond and O'Connor have argued, chapters 11-20 serve to explain the fall of the southern kingdom. This function works on a number of levels. The chapters illustrate the guilt of Judah in general terms. Furthermore, the chapters prepare the audience for the naming of the guilty parties. The rhetorical strategy for this illustration is forceful. Chapters 11-20 dramatize the guilt of the enemies in great detail, but leave them largely nameless. Through this mode of presentation, the audience is predisposed to accept the guilt of the enemies before their identity is unveiled, which takes place beginning in chapter 20 and is advanced in great detail in chapters 21-25 (see Diamond 1987:174).

There is another function of chapters 11-20 related to their larger context. Chapters 7-25 help to explain the fall of the southern kingdom through the figure of the prophet himself. Jeremiah was not only the spokesman of Yahweh. His life also paralleled the life of the nation in crisis. As Childs (1979:350) has observed, the "prophet not only consistently warned of the coming divine judgement, but he participated himself in the judgement of his people." Thrust into the rapid decline of the late Judean monarchy, Jeremiah suffered the events of his day with the people. He witnessed the raging issues of his times, suffered humiliation at the people's hands and went into exile. This parallelism of Jeremiah and Israel is not simply a general impression inferred from their comparable fates; the language applied to both the prophet and Jerusalem in chapters 13-15 may indicate a deliberate comparison of the prophet and the people. The relationship between Jeremiah and Israel is also a reflection of theological "cause and effect": because Israel treated Jeremiah in such a negative fashion, in a sense "exiled" him within his own land, so Israel will be treated by Jeremiah's divine patron. Diamond (1987:142; cf. 51) comments on how the apparent failure of the prophetic mission replicates the relationship between Yahweh and Israel: "The defeat of the prophet in his struggle with his mission provides the basis for the sure defeat of the nation in its struggle against the prophetic word." The prophet's persecution parallels Yahweh's abuse by Israel (Diamond 1987:153, 156; M. S. Smith 1987b).

Commentators on the book of Jeremiah have attributed further significance to the prophet's life for Israel (von Rad 1983; Polk 1984). His life functions as more than an explanation for the fall of the southern king-

---

[4] For a different reading of chapters 21-25 in connection with chapters 11-20, see O'Connor 1988:146-48.

dom. The prophet's life becomes paradigmatic for the community after its fall in 587. Budde (1899:198-99) made essentially the same point in suggesting that Jeremiah was a prototype for Israel:

> And, as a matter of fact, the future advance of Israel on this general line follows in the footsteps of Jeremiah...All the patience, all the godliness, which Israel matured in the midst of the sufferings of actual life, finds its prototype in our prophet. Thus the very same man who stood as "a pillar of iron and a wall of brass" *against* his people during his lifetime (i. 18, xv. 20) became after his death "a pillar of iron and a wall of brass" *for* his people. (Budde's italics)

The identification between the fates of both prophet and enemies offered a note of hope. Jeremiah's ongoing call for the demise of the people in his laments and the series of divine responses, sometimes assurance, sometimes challenge, sometimes divine persecution, represent the ambiguities of Israel's life with Yahweh. Jeremiah's words end in chapter 20 not by proclaiming divine goodness or salvation (see O'Connor 1988:76). Rather, in 20:7-13 the prophet curses his own life and mission. This apparent expression of despair provides substantial hope for the audience that transmitted the prophet's words, because like the prophet, they experienced pain, judgement, persecution, abandonment. The life of Jeremiah perhaps served as a model in that the suffering evidenced in the laments could provide some solace to a people in exile and recovering from exile (cf. Brueggemann 1987:128-29).

The paradigmatic character of Jeremiah's life perhaps provided a modicum of hope insofar as the prophet who suffered so enormously was the same prophet on whose lips the people heard the words of consolation occasionally expressed in the book named after the prophet. There are expressions of hope appearing at various points in chapters 11-20. Jer 12:15, 16:14-15 and 17:24-26 belong to prose pieces offering hope, yet the consolation expressed is conditional in character. The book of Jeremiah largely sounds the death knell of the southern kingdom, and chapters 11-20 recapitulate this event on a variety of levels — in announcing the event, in placing blame for the event, in asserting the impact of the event on Yahweh, and in recapitulating the event through the life of the prophet. The dominant theme of chapters 11-20 remains one of judgement. Indeed, the presentation of the prophet in context is subordinate to this purpose (Diamond 1987:183; Carroll 1989:113). Chapters 11-20 partake of the theme of judgement dominant throughout the book of Jeremiah. Although there are sections of consolation such as chapters 30-

31 and 33, the book of Jeremiah remains fundamentally a book about judgement. Furthermore, the book contains no major section of restoration oracles like Isaiah 40-66 or Ezekiel 40-48. Rather, the book ends with exile.

Bibliography

Aejmelaeus, A.
1986   "Function and Interpretation of כִּי in Biblical Hebrew." *JBL* 105:193-209.

Ahuis, F.
1982   *Der Klagende Gerichtsprophet: Studien zur Klage in der Überlieferung von der altestamentlichen Gerichtspropheten.* Stuttgart: Calwer.

Avishur, Y.
1984   *Stylistic Studies of Word-Pairs in Biblical and Ancient Semitic Literatures.* AOAT 210. Kevelaer: Verlag Butzon & Bercker; Neukirchen-Vluyn: Neukirchener Verlag.

Barthélemy, D.
1986   *Critique Textuelle de l'Ancien Testament; 2. Isaïe, Jérémie, Lamentations.* OBO 50/2. Fribourg: Éditions Universitaires; Göttingen: Vandenhoeck & Ruprecht.

Baumgartner, W.
1988   *Jeremiah's Poems of Lament.* Trans. D. E. Orton. Sheffield: Almond.

Begrich, J.
1938   *Studien zu Deuterojesajas.* BWANT 77. Stuttgart: Kohlhammer.

Blank, S.
1948   "The Confessions of Jeremiah and the Meaning of Prayer." *HUCA* 21:331-54.

Bloch-Smith, E. M.
1990   "Judahite Burial Practices and Beliefs about the Dead." Ph.D. dissertation, University of Chicago.

Bright, J.
1951   "The Date of the Prose Sermons of Jeremiah." *JBL* 70:15-55.
1965   *Jeremiah.* AB 21. Garden City, NY: Doubleday.

Brueggemann, W. A.
1973　　"Jeremiah's Use of Rhetorical Questions." *JBL* 92:358-74.
1987　　"The Book of Jeremiah: Portrait of the Prophet." In Mays and Achtemeier 1987:113-29 = *Interpretation* 37 (1983) 130-45.

Budde, K.
1899　　*Religion of Israel to the Exile.* American Lectures on the History of Religions, Fourth Series - 1898-1899. New York/London: G. P. Putnam's Sons/The Knickerbocker Press.

Callaway, P.
1986　　"Source Criticism of the Temple Scroll." *RevQ* 46 = 12/2:213-22.

Carroll, R. P.
1986　　*Jeremiah.* OTL. Philadelphia: Westminster.
1989　　*Jeremiah.* Old Testament Guides. Sheffield: JSOT.

Childs, B. S.
1979　　*Introduction to the Old Testament as Scripture.* Philadelphia: Fortress.

Clines, D. J. A., and D. M. Gunn
1976　　"Form, Occasion, and Redaction in Jeremiah 20." *ZAW* 88:390-409.
1978　　"'You Tried to Persuade Me' and 'Violence! Outrage!' in Jeremiah xx 7-8." *VT* 28:20-27.

Cooper, A.
1987　　"On Reading Biblical Poetry." *Maarav* 4/2:221-41.

Cornhill, C. H.
1905　　*Das Buch Jeremiah.* Leipzig: Tauchnitz.

Crenshaw, J. L.
1985　　"Education in Ancient Israel." *JBL* 104:601-15.

Darr, K. P.
1989　　"Write or True? A Response to Ellen Francis Davis." *Signs and Wonders; Biblical Texts in Literary Focus.* Ed. J. C. Exum. Semeia Studies. n.p.: Scholars. 239-47.

Davis, E.
1989　　"Swallowing Hard: Reflections on Ezekiel's Dumbness." *Signs and Wonders; Biblical Texts in Literary Focus.* Ed. J. C. Exum. Semeia Studies. n.p.: Scholars. 217-37.

Diamond, A. R.
1987   *The Confessions of Jeremiah in Context; Scenes of Prophetic Drama.* JSOTSup45. Sheffield: JSOT Press.
1989   Review of K. M. O'Connor, *The Confessions of Jeremiah: Their Interpretation and Role in Chapters 1-25. JBL* 108:694-96.

Duhm, B.
1901   *Das Buch Jeremia erklärt.* KAT XI. Tübingen: J. C. B. Mohr.

Ehrman, A.
1960   "A Note on בשׁח in Jer. 12:5." *JSS* 5:153-55.

Eissfeldt, O.
1965   *The Old Testament; An Introduction.* Trans. P. R. Ackroyd. New York/Evanston.

Fisher, L. R.
1963   "The Temple Quarter." *JSS* 8:34-41.

Fitzgerald, A.
1972   "The Mythological Background for the Presentation of Jerusalem as a Queen and False Worship as Adultery in the OT." *CBQ* 34:403-16.
1975   "*BTWLT* and *BT* as Titles for Capital Cities." *CBQ* 37:167-83.

Fretheim, T. E.
1987   "The Repentence of God: A Study of Jeremiah 18:7-10." *Hebrew Annual Review* 11:81-92.

Galling, K.
1956   "Die Ausrufung des Namens als Rechtsakt in Israel." *TLZ* 81:65-70.

Gitay, Y.
1980   "Deutero-Isaiah: Oral or Written?" *JBL* 99:185-97.

Gwaltney, W. C.
1983   "The Biblical Book of Lamentations in the Context of Near Eastern Lament Literature." *Scripture in Context II; More Essays on the Comparative Method.* Eds. W. W. Hallo, J. C. Moyer and L. G. Perdue. Winona Lake, IN: Eisenbrauns. 191-211.

Haran, M.
1988   "On the Diffusion of Literacy and Schools in Ancient Israel."
        Congress Volume; Jerusalem 1986. Ed. J. Emerton. VTSup 40.
        Leiden: Brill. 81-95.

Held, M.
1965   "The Action-Result (Factitive-Passive) Sequence of Identical
        Verbs in Biblical Hebrew and Ugaritic." *JBL* 84:272-82.
1973   "Pits and Pitfalls in Akkadian and in Biblical Hebrew." *JANES*
        5:173-90.

Heschel, A. J.
1962   *The Prophets*. New York/Evanston: Harper & Row.

Holladay, W. L.
1964   "The Background of Jeremiah's Self-Understanding: Moses,
        Samuel, and Psalm 22." *JBL* 83:153-64.
1966   "Jeremiah and Moses: Further Observations." *JBL* 85:111-13.
1976   *The Architecture of Jeremiah 1-20*. Lewisburg, PA: Bucknell
        University.
1986   *Jeremiah 1; A Commentary on the Book of the Prophet Jeremiah.
        Chapters 1-25*. Hermeneia. Philadelphia: Fortress.

Hubmann, F. D.
1978   *Untersuchungen zu den Konfession: Jer 11:18-12:6 und der Jer 15:10-
        21*. Echter: Echter Verlag.
1984   "Stationen einer Berufung: Die 'Konfessionen' Jeremias." *TPQ*
        1:25-39.

Hyatt, J. P.
1944   "The Original Text of Jeremiah 11 15-16." *JBL* 63:57-60.
1951   "The Deuteronomic Edition of Jeremiah." *Vanderbilt Studies in
        the Humanities I*. Ed. R. C. Beatty, J. P. Hyatt and M. K. Spears.
        Nashville, TN: Vanderbilt University. 71-95.

Ittmann, N.
1981   *Die Konfessionen Jeremias: Ihre Bedeutung für die Verkündigung des
        Propheten*. Neukirchen-Vluyn: Neukirchener Verlag.

Janzen, J. G.
1973   *Studies in the Text of Jeremiah*. Cambridge, MA: Harvard
        University.

Kelly, F. T.
1920 "The Imperfect with Simple Waw." *JBL* 29:1-23.

Kesterson, J. C.
1986 "Cohortative and Short Imperfect Forms in *Serakim* and *Dam. Doc.*" *RevQ* 47 = 12/3:369-82.

Koch, K.
1983 "Is There a Doctrine of Retribution in the Old Testament?" *Theodicy in the Old Testament.* Ed. J. L. Crenshaw. Tr. T. H. Trapp. Philadelphia: Fortress; London: SPCK. 57-87.

Kopf, L.
1958 "Arabische Etymologien und Parallelen zum Bibelwörterbuch." *VT* 8:101-215.

Lauha, R.
1983 *Psychophysicher Sprachgebrauch im Alten Testament. Eine strukturalsemantische Analyse von lb, npš und rwḥ.* Annales Scientarum Fennicae, Dissertationes Humanarum Litterarum 35. Helsinki: Suomalainen Tiedeakatemia.

Leclerq, J.
1954 "Les 'Confessions' de Jérémie." In P. Béguere, J. Leclerq and J. Steinmann. *Etudes sur les prophètes d'Israël.* Lectio Divina 14. Paris: Cerf. 111-45.

Lemaire, A.
1981 *Les écoles et la formation de la Bible dans l'ancien Israël.* OBO 39. Fribourg: Editions Universitaires; Göttingen: Vandenhoeck & Ruprecht.

Levenson, J.
1984 "Some Unnoticed Connotations in Jeremiah 20:9." *CBQ* 46: 223-25.

Levine, B.
1978 "The Temple Scroll; Aspects of its Historical Provenance and Literary Character." *BASOR* 232:5-23.

Loisy, A.
1910 *The Religion of Israel.* Trans. A. Galton. New York: G. P. Putnam's Sons.

Lundbom, J. R.
1975   *Jeremiah: A Study in Ancient Hebrew Rhetoric.* SBLDS 18. Missoula, MT: Scholars.

MacDonald, B.
1975   "Some Distinctive Features of Israelite Spoken Hebrew." *BO* 33:162-75.

McKane, W.
1981   "Relations between Poetry and Prose in the Book of Jeremiah with Special Reference to Jeremiah III 6-11 and XII 14-17." *Congress Volume; Vienna 1980.* VTSup 32. Ed. J. A. Emerton. Leiden: Brill. 220-37.
1986   *A Critical and Exegetical Commentary on Jeremiah. Volume I; Introduction and Commentary on Jeremiah I-XXV.* ICC. Edinburgh: T. & T. Clark.

Mays, J. L. and P. J. Achtemeier, ed.
1987   *Interpreting the Prophets.* Philadelphia: Fortress.

Meek, T. J.
1955-1956   "Result and Purpose Clauses in Hebrew." *JQR* 45-46:40-43.

Melamed, E. Z.
1961   "Break-up of Stereotype Phrases as an Artistic Device in Biblical Hebrew." *Scripta Hierosolymitana* 8:115-153.

Mendenhall, G. E.
1973   *The Tenth Generation; The Origins of the Biblical Tradition.* Baltimore/London: Johns Hopkins.

Millard, A. R.
1987   "The Question of Israelite Literacy." *Bible Review* 3/3:22-31.

de Moor, J. C.
1987   *An Anthology of Religious Texts from Ugarit.* Nisaba 16. Leiden: Brill.

Mowinckel, S.
1914   *Zur Komposition des Buches Jeremia.* Videnskapsselskapets Skrifter II. Hist.-folis. Klasse 1913 No 5. Kristiana: Jacob Dybwad.

Muraoka, T.
1985   *Emphatic Words and Structures in Biblical Hebrew.* Jerusalem: Magnes; Leiden: Brill.

O'Connor, K. M.
1988   *The Confessions of Jeremiah: Their Interpretation and Role in Chapters 1-25.* SBLDS 94. Atlanta, GA: Scholars.
1989   "'Do Not Trim a Word': The Contributions of Chapter 26 to the Book of Jeremiah." *CBQ* 51:617-30.

del Olmo Lete, G.
1971   "La unidad literaria de Jer. 14-17." *EstBíb* 30:3-46.

Orlinsky, H. M.
1940-41/1941-42 "On the Cohortative and the Jussive after an Imperative or Interjection in Biblical Hebrew." *JQR* 31:371-82, 32:191-205, 273-77.

Overholt, T.
1988   "Jeremiah." *Harper's Bible Commentary.* Ed. J. L. Mays. San Francisco: Harper & Row. 597-645.

Pardee, D.
1988   *Les textes para-mythologiques de la 24e campagne (1961).* Ras Shamra - Ougarit IV. Editions Recherche sur les Civilisations, Mémoire 77. Paris: Editions Recherche sur les Civilisations.

Parker, S. B.
1988   "The Birth Announcement." *Ascribe to the Lord; Biblical & other studies in memory of Peter C. Craigie.* Ed. L. Eslinger & G. Taylor. JSOTSup 67. Sheffield: JSOT. 133-49.

Paul, S.
1969   "Literary and Ideological Echoes of Jeremiah in Deutero-Isaiah." *Proceedings of the Fifth World Congress of Jewish Studies.* Volume I. Ed. P. Peli. Jerusalem: World Union of Jewish Studies. 102-20.

Pitard, W.
1982   "Akkadian *ekēmu* and Hebrew *nāqam.*" *Maarav* 3/1:5-25

Pohlmann, K. F.
1989   *Die Ferne Gottes - Studien zum Jeremiabuch: Beiträge zu den "Konfessionen" im Jeremiabuch und ein Versuch zur Frage nach den Anfängen der Jeremiatradition.* BZAW 179. Berlin/New York: Walter de Gruyter.

Polk, T.
1984   *The Prophetic Persona; Jeremiah and the Language of Self.* JSOTSup 20. Sheffield: JSOT.

Pope, M. H.
1953   "'Pleonastic' Waw before Nouns in Ugaritic and Hebrew." *JAOS* 73:95-98.

Propp, W. H.
1987   "On Hebrew *śāde(h)*, 'Highland'." *VT* 37:230-233.

von Rad, G.
1965   *Old Testament Theology*. Volume 1. Trans. J. G. Stalker. New York: Harper and Row.
1983   "The Confessions of Jeremiah." *Theodicy in the Old Testament*. Ed. J. L. Crenshaw. Tr. A. Ehlin. Philadelphia: Fortress; London: SPCK. 88-99.

Robert, A.
1943   "Jérémie et la Réforme deutéronomique d'après Jér. XI, 1-14." *RSR* 5-16.

Rudolph, W.
1968   *Jeremia*. Third ed. HAT I, 12. Tübingen: J. C. B. Mohr.

Running, L. G.
1985   "A Study of the Relationship of the Syriac Version to the Massoretic Hebrew, Targum Jonathan, and Septuagint Texts in Jeremiah 18." *Biblical and Related Studies presented to Samuel Iwry*. Ed. A. Kort and S. Morschauer. Winona Lake, IN: Eisenbrauns. 227-35.

Seitz, C. R.
1985   "The Crisis of Interpretation over the Meaning and Purpose of the Exile; A redactional study of Jeremiah xxi-xliii." *VT* 35:78-97.
1989a   "The Prophet Moses and the Canonical Shape of Jeremiah." *ZAW* 101:3-27.
1989b   *Theology in Conflict; Reactions to the Exile in the Book of Jeremiah*. BZAW 176. Berlin/New York: Walter de Gruyter.

Skinner, J.
1922   *Prophecy and Religion: Studies in the Life of Jeremiah*. Cambridge: Cambridge University.

Smith, G. V.
1979   "The Use of Quotations in Jeremiah XV 11-14." *VT* 29:229-31.

Smith, M. S.
1987a   "Death in Jeremiah IX, 20." *UF* 19:289-93.
1987b   "Jeremiah IX 9 - A Divine Lament." *VT* 37:97-99.

Soderlund, S.
1985   *The Greek Text of Jeremiah; A Revised Hypothesis.* JSOTSup 47.
        Sheffield: JSOT.

Stegemann, H.
1983a   "'Das Land' in der Tempelrolle und in anderen Texten aus den
        Qumranfunden." *Das Land Israel in biblischer Zeit; Jerusalem-
        Symposium 1981 der Hebräischen Universität und der Georg-August-
        Universität.* Ed. G. Strecker. Göttingen: Vandenhoeck &
        Ruprecht. 154-71.
1983b   "Die Bedeutung der Qumranfunde für die Erforschung der
        Apokalyptik." *Apocalypticism in the Mediterranean World and the
        Near East; Proceedings of the International Colloquium on
        Apocalypticism, Uppsala, August 12-17, 1979.* Ed. D. Hellholm.
        Tübingen: J. C. B. Mohr. 495-530.
1985   "Some Aspects of Eschatology in Texts from the Qumran
        Community and in the Teachings of Jesus." *Biblical Archaeology
        Today; Proceedings of the International Congress on Biblical
        Archaeology. Jerusalem, April 1984.* Jerusalem: Israel Exploration
        Society. 408-26.

Stulman, L.
1985   *The Other Text of Jeremiah; A Reconstruction of the Hebrew Text
        underlying the Greek Version of the Prose Sections of Jeremiah with
        English Translation.* Lanham/New York/London: University
        Press of America.
1986   *The Prose Sermons of the Book of Jeremiah; A Redescription of the
        Correspondences with the Deuteronomistic Literature in the Light of
        Recent Text-critical Research.* SBLDS 83. Atlanta: Scholars.
1989   Review of A. R. Diamond, *The Confessions of Jeremiah in Context:
        Scenes of Prophetic Drama. CBQ* 51:316-18.

Thiel, W.
1973   *Die deuteronomistische Redaktion von Jeremia 1-25.* WMANT 41.
        Neukirchen-Vluyn: Neukirchener Verlag.
1981   *Die deuteronomistische Redaktion von Jeremia 26-45.* WMANT 52.
        Neukirchen-Vluyn: Neukirchener Verlag.

Tov, E.
1972   "L'incidence de la critique textuelle sur la critique littéraire dans le Livre de Jérémie." *RB* 79:189-99.
1981   "Some Aspects of the Textual and Literary History of the Book of Jeremiah." *Le Livre de Jérémie: le prophète et son milieu, les oracles et leur transmission.* Ed. P. M. Bogaert. BETL LIV. Leuven: Uitgeverij Peeters. 145-67.
1985   "The Literary History of the Book of Jeremiah in the Light of Its Textual History." *Empirical Models for Biblical Criticism.* Ed. J. H. Tigay. Philadelphia: University of Pennsylvania. 211-37.

Unterman, J.
1987   *From Repentance to Redemption. Jeremiah's Thought in Transition.* JSOTSup 54. Sheffield: JSOT.

Varughese, A.
1984   "The Hebrew Text Underlying the Old Greek Translation of Jeremiah 10-20." Ph.D. dissertation, Drew University.

Vermeylen, J.
1981   "Essai de Redaktionsgeschichte des <<Confessions de Jérémie>>." *Le Livre de Jérémie: le prophète et son milieu, les oracles et leur transmission.* Ed. P. M. Bogaert. BETL LIV. Leuven: Uitgeverij Peeters. 239-70.

Volz, P.
1922   *Der Prophet Jeremia.* KAT X. Leipzig: A. Deichertsche Verlagsbuchhandlung D. Werner Scholl.

van Waldow, H. E.
1989   Review of A. R. Diamond, *The Confessions of Jeremiah in Context. JBL* 108:125-27.

Weinfeld, M.
1976   "Jeremiah and the Spiritual Metamorphosis of Israel." *ZAW* 88:17-55.

Weippert, H.
1973   *Die Prosareden der Jeremiabuches.* BZAW 132. Berlin/New York: Walter de Gruyter.

Wilhelmi, G.
1975   "Weg mit den vielen Altären! (Jeremia xi, 15)." *VT* 25:119-21.

Wilson, R. R.
1980   *Prophecy and Society in Ancient Israel*. Philadelphia: Fortress.
1988a   "The Community of Second Isaiah." *Reading and Preaching the Book of Isaiah*. Ed. C. R. Seitz. Philadelphia: Fortress. 53-70.
1988b   "Ezekiel." *Harper's Bible Commentary*. Ed. J. L. Mays. San Francisco: Harper & Row. 652-94.

Winckler, H.
1893   *Altorientalische Forschungen III*. Leipzig: Verlag von Eduard Pfeiffer.

Wolff, H. W.
1974   *Anthropology of the Old Testament*. Trans. M. Kohl. Philadelphia: Fortress.

Yadin, Y.
1983   *The Temple Scroll*. 3 vols. Jerusalem: The Israel Exploration Society/The Institute of Archaeology of the Hebrew University of Jerusalem/The Shrine of the Book.

Index of Textual Citations

Index of Scholars Cited

Index of Subjects